A COUNTRY CALLED
NIGERIA

The Journey of an African American Businessman
Who Lived in Nigeria for More Than Fourteen Years

Robert Siller, Jr.

To order additional copies of this book, contact:
Xlibris Corporation
1-888-795-4274
www.Xlibris.com
Orders@Xlibris.com
42414

A COUNTRY CALLED
NIGERIA

Contents

To my wife, Uloma and all the other people that make up "A Country Called Nigeria".

CORRECTIONS

Page 18...Should read 1978 instead of 1998.

The following two sentences precede the red mark:

Page 130..."Since the AIDS virus was spreading mainly through heterosexual contact in Africa, the majority of deaths could have been avoided if the use of condoms had been encouraged. Unfortunately, Bush's administration paid more attention to abstinence only and less interest on the use of condoms.

Phonetic Pronunciation of Nigerian and Other African Names

Abacha	ah-ba-cha
Abiola	ah-be-o-la
Abuja	ah-boo-ja
Ada	ah-da
Ade	ah-day
Alhaji	al-ha-gee
akara	ah-ca-ra
Arochuka	are-row-chu-ka
Asari	ah-sa-re
Awolowo	ah-wo-la-wo
Azikiwe	ah-zek-e-way
Babangida	ba-ban-gee-da
Benue	ben-way
Biafra	be-af-ra
Buhari	boo-ha-re
buka	boo-ka
Bumi	boo-me
Chidi	che-dee
dashiki	da-shi-kee
Enugu	e-new-gu
Fela	fel-la
Fulani	foo-la-nee
Hausa	how-za
Ibadan	e-ba-don
Igbobi	e-bo-be
Ibo	e-bo
Ijaw	e-jaw
Ikeja	e-ka-ja
Ikorudu	e-cu-ra-du
Ikoyi	e-co-ye

Ironsi	e-run-see
Mbeki	um-beck-e
Kuti	koo-tee
molue	moe-way
niara	ni-ra
Obasanjo	o-ba-son-joe
Oga	o-ga
Ogba	og-ba
Ojota	o-jo-ta
Ojukwu	o-jook-ooh
Ole	o-lay
Olu	o-lou
Otukpo	o-to-po
Saro-Wiwa	sa-row-we-wa
Shagari	sha-ga-ree
Sharia	sha-re-ya
Shonekan	sho-nec-con
Soyinka	sho-yin-ka
Taiwo	tie-wo
Urohobo	u-row-bo
Uloma	ooh-lo-ma
Yinka	yin-ka
Yoruba	u-ra-ba

Introduction

This story is about an African American businessman who embarked on what he thought would be a promising business trip to Nigeria in 1978. Although that first business trip was unsuccessful, he would eventually make four more trips, with the hope that the next trip would bring him that elusive financial success. I am that African American businessman, and in the process of making these trips, I lived in the country for more than fourteen years. My experiences included living under military rule, a strained union, corruption, and other social problems. Despite these difficulties, I had the opportunity of sharing the warm and friendly relationships with members of the three major ethnic groups (Hausa, Ibo, and Yoruba) and some of the over 250 minorities.

Before I continue with this journey, it is important that I tell you something about myself and what inspired me to write this book. I was less than a year old in 1944 when my parents left the rural community of Richwood, Louisiana, in search of better employment and living conditions. Their search led them to Alameda, California, an island city in the San Francisco/Oakland Bay Area. Like the majority of African American families, our family was held together with love, faith, determination, and a desire to make the best of any given situation. From this lifestyle, I developed a character of goodwill through my mother and the strength of my father to support this goodwill.

We lived in one of several projects on the west end of Alameda that was built during the war years to help house the numerous workers employed by the defense agencies in the Bay Area. Our social environment in the estuary projects was mixed with segregated housing and an integrated school system. Thanks to my parents, I spent very little time thinking about our semisegregated living conditions. After having said that, I am liberal enough not to rain on someone else's parade, and conservative enough not to let anyone rain on mind. After graduating from high school in 1961, I worked odd jobs until I received my draft notice from the U.S. Army in 1962. My brother, who was drafted in 1952, advised me to enlist because I had a better chance of choosing my school and duty station. So I enlisted in 1963 and was able to get my school of choice in communications and served the majority of my time in Germany.

I married shortly after my discharged in 1967, and although the marriage lasted only a few years, we were fortunate to have a wonderful daughter. From 1967 to 1977, I worked the majority of that time as a data communications operator for the U.S. Civil Service. I graduated from Laney Junior College in 1974 and in the process developed a new awareness of the African continent. But because the focus was on South Africa, very little attention was given to Nigeria, with the exception of their civil war (1967-1970) and that the country was under military rule.

For the next three years, I continued enjoying the social and economic benefits of the civil rights movements led by Dr. Martin Luther King Jr. in the 1950s and 1960s. With this in mind, I decided to take a chance on business in 1977 and became the co-owner of a sporting-goods store in East Oakland. In the beginning, the business was a success, but greed and the lack of accountability cause the partnership to fail and eventually led to the downfall of the store in 1978.

Prior to my experiences in Nigeria, I had no ambitions of becoming a writer. However, after witnessing their unnecessary suffering and listening to Nigerians complaining about their situation, I knew I had to try and help get their story out with whatever resources I had at my disposal.

It is important to note that the African continent is full of rich cultures and natural resources. But the slave trade, colonization, and the systematic rape of the continent had placed unnecessary obstacles in the path of nation building. It was not only an uphill task for African leaders to lead after their independence but to also rectify what their former colonial masters had destroyed in an attempt to enlighten what they perceived to be an unenlightened continent. With the exception of African countries gaining their independence and Nelson Mandela becoming South Africa's president, there has been very little positive news from the continent.

In the past, Nigeria was known as the giant of Africa because of the country's great potential in natural and human resources. But the discovery of oil in 1956 and its subsequent boom in the early 1970s has turned out to be more of a curse than a blessing to the people of Nigeria. Despite the abundance of natural and human resources, the majority of Nigerians have not been able to enjoy the basic benefits derived from these resources. Instead of being one of the wealthiest countries in the world, it is one of the poorest. Another one of Nigeria's problems is the social situation, and it left me wondering why the British colonial government would bring the north and south together in 1914 without any concern for their social and culture backgrounds. This lack of concern, had played a major role in causing confusion and dissension between the two regions.

After witnessing Nigeria's problems for more than fourteen years, it left me with a strong urge to write about their situation in a constructive way. My journey touched on various levels of the Nigerian society, and I would like to share these experiences with you in *A Country Called Nigeria*.

Chapter One

Doing Business with Olu

My Nigerian journey began on a Friday in July 1978 when my former teacher and athletic coach, Mr. Don Grant, told me about a Nigerian who wanted to purchase basketball uniforms for a military team in Nigeria. During our phone conversation, Mr. Grant also informed me that Nigeria was rich in oil and other natural resources. This was good compared to my situation, which included a failed partnership and the possibility of my business going bankrupt. I told Mr. Grant that I was looking forward to meeting his Nigerian friend, and we agreed to meet in the store the following morning.

Around ten o'clock the next morning, Mr. Grant came to the store and introduced me to Mr. Olu Williams and Angela, his Italian American wife. I wondered about Olu's last name before quickly remembering that Nigeria was formerly a British colony. I was impressed with the way the Nigerian walked through the front door, neatly dressed in a traditional starched, three-piece white caftan suit, tastefully trimmed with gold embroidery, and a pair of white Italian slip-on shoes. Olu was about five and a half feet tall and built solidly, with an ebony complexion and an outgoing personality to match his attire.

He complimented me on the store and seemed quite impressed that an African American was the owner. As we began our meeting, Olu repeated what Mr. Grant had told me about the country. He went on to say that the country is made up of three major ethnic groups. I asked which ethnic group he belonged to, and he said, "I am Yoruba, and our ethnic group is from the western part of Nigeria. The other two ethnic groups are the Hausas in the north and Ibos in the east, and over 250 minorities spread throughout the country."

I was impressed by his description of Nigeria and even more impressed when he said, "Mr. Grant has told me that you can supply basketball uniforms and tennis shoes." I told him yes as he continued," I wanted to know if you could prepare an order for ten sets of basketball uniforms with the shoes."

He said the order was for a Nigerian military team and that he only had three weeks to prepare the uniforms for shipment. Although the store was struggling, I had enough inventory to complete the order. But I told Olu I would need specifications and sizes.

Olu took a folded paper from the inside pocket of his caftan suit and said, "We didn't have time to have the specifications typed like the letter, but it's official order from the military government."

Outside of the specifications being handwritten, it had all the requirements: silk screening, shoe sizes, and uniforms in the country's colors of green and white. After providing him with an estimate cost of about $500, he said that he would be able to pay me with a cashier's check within thirty days after the goods arrived in Lagos. Because of Olu's association with Mr. Grant and the potential for future business, we were able to seal the deal with a handshake.

The order was ready two weeks later, and once again I could tell Olu was impressed, especially after I told him that I had included some extra items (head and wristbands and a couple of deflated basketballs) in an effort to show my goodwill. Two days later, Olu called to inform me that I should prepare for a business trip to Nigeria that coming September because he knew the army would offer me an invitation. Traveling to Nigeria had never entered my mind, but I was receptive to the idea. He also told me that he would not be taking the package to Nigeria and that his associate Bob Chang would pick it up the following morning. He said the package would be passed on to another associate who was traveling to Lagos that following evening.

The next day, Bob Chang, a Chinese American, came by to pick up the package. In our brief conversation, he said he was an architect by profession and that he and Olu were trying to sell portable housing units to the Nigerian government. I told him that I might be going to Nigeria soon, and he indicated that it was likely that we would see each other in Lagos.

Olu left for Nigeria in August 1998 and said that he would return in about thirty days. With the order behind me, I began the process to get my passport and immunizations against yellow fever, malaria, and cholera. While I was waiting for Olu to return from Nigeria, I attempted to get additional information on the country, and I was able to do this through the Oakland Public Library. Geographically, Nigeria is located in West Africa, with Niger on the northern border, Republic of Benin to the west, Cameroon on the east, and its southern shores touch the Gulf of Guinea. The country gained its independence from the British in 1960, and its population of more than seventy million people is the largest in Africa. It is about twice the size of California, and the climate ranges from semidesert in the north to arid and humid in the south. Like other African countries, Nigeria has two seasons: the rainy season between April and October and the dry season from October to March, which is often accompanied by the Harmattan (dry, dusty winds that blow from the Sahara desert). I was amazed at the abundance of Nigeria's natural resources, such as oil deposits and natural gas. The country is agriculturally blessed with vegetables, spices, palm products, cocoa, coffee, sugar, peanuts, cotton, rubber, and more. The country's wildlife population was in decline because of hunting, agriculture, and population growth. The city of Lagos is the federal capital of Nigeria and is the center of economic activity in the country. Unfortunately, this brief course in Nigerian history was not enough to prepare me for what I was about to experience, which included the lack of accountability, a corrupt elite class, constant incursion of the military into Nigerian politics, religious and ethnic intolerance.

True to his word, Olu returned about a month later, and I was promptly given a cashier's check and was told that the order and gifts were well received. A few days later, Olu accompanied me to the Nigerian Consulate in San Francisco to apply for my business visa. From the receptionist to the visa officer, I was offered courteous and efficient service. My initial impression of Nigeria through Olu and the consulate only gave me a greater desire to visit the country. I left my passport, and three days later it was ready with a ninety-day business visa. I once again discussed this business opportunity with my brother, also the store manager, and we agreed that because of the store's fragile financial situation, Nigeria was worth taking a risk. Mr. Grant felt the Nigerian venture would open up unlimited opportunities, and the only way to find out was to go there.

As we approached our departure date, I asked Olu about the army's letter of invitation. He stated that it was an oral invitation. I had doubts about the invitation, but with a completed order behind me, I decided to overlook it. In September 1978, Olu and I set off for Nigeria from San Francisco. After flying for about eleven hours with a layover in New York we arrived in London about 6:00 AM, and after clearing immigration, we took the Underground Railroad to the heart of the city. We checked into a small hotel, and I enjoyed seeing the new sights, including Big Ben and Buckingham Palace. We spent the rest of the day visiting friends of Olu.

That evening we checked out of the hotel and headed for Heathrow Airport for our late-night flight to Nigeria. When we reached the check-in counter, my impression was that some of the Nigerian passengers returning to Nigeria were relocating after a long stay because of the amount of luggage they had.

Olu said with a broad grin, "Some of these passengers will be back in a month or two with the same amount of luggage, if not more, because they are carrying items for resale in Nigeria."

We were on the final leg of our journey, and as we taxied onto the runway, I took note of the cabin crew, who were smartly dressed in their country's trimmed white and green uniforms. After flying for about five hours, the captain notified the passengers of our descent, and I started mentally preparing myself for the experience of a lifetime. We taxied to a rectangular one-story building that served as the terminal.

I could also see construction work taking place in the distance, and Olu said proudly, "That's the new international airport, and it will be ready in a couple of years. The new airport was named after Murtala Mohammed, who died in an attempted military coup in 1976."

As I prepared my passport and health card, Olu said, "Let me have your passport; we can save time by doing it my way."

We disembarked from the plane directly onto the tarmac. The tropical morning air took my air-conditioned lungs with a breath of surprise. A shuttle bus took us to the terminal, and as we lined up to go through immigrations and customs, Olu caught the attention of an immigration staff and motioned for him to come over. His uniform was patterned after the British style, and like Olu's last name, it reminded me of the country's colonial history.

Olu shook hands, spoke Yoruba to the immigration staff, and discreetly handed him our passports and health records. The immigration employee asked us to follow him to the front of the line where we waited alongside a cubical raised platform as immigration officials screened and processed other incoming passengers. While Olu was talking and joking with the immigration officials, I felt uncomfortable for jumping the line over those who were waiting patiently.

Within minutes, one of the officers turned and said, "Welcome to Nigeria," as he returned our passports and health cards. Olu had obviously facilitated our processing by doing things his way. Being accustomed to tipping after a service, I was now experiencing the custom of tipping prior to service.

The next step was to collect our bags and clear customs. I watched as a few incoming passengers tried unsuccessfully to convince customs officials that the extra items in their suitcases were for personal use. As we waited for our luggage, a senior customs officer walked up to Olu and said in pidgin English, "O-boy, how now, you don't return."

They shook hands, and Olu told me later that the word *don't* in pidgin English literally means *yes* in English. We retrieved our luggage, and it was our turn to be asked if we had anything to declare by the customs officer.

Olu's senior customs friend intervened and said, "These two gentlemen are okay, and we shouldn't delay them any further."

Olu had once again facilitated our movement through customs, and I was quickly learning how to navigate within Nigerian society.

We were now standing in front of the airport when a taxi driver approached Olu and said, "Good morning, *oga*, would you like to hire a taxi?"

Olu said, "How much to Victoria Island?"

The taxi driver said, "Fifty naira."

Olu replied, "That's too much. I will give you ten naira for the journey."

In a bargaining society like Nigeria, there is generally no set price for anything. The buyer bargains for the lowest while the seller tries for the highest, and somewhere in between the two parties come to an agreement.

Olu and the driver settled on a price, and as we climbed into the taxi, Olu sensed my curiosity with the word *oga* and said, "*Oga* is a Yoruba word for *sir*, and of course you know the meaning for *madam*."

As we made our way to Victoria Island, newspaper vendors were walking and running alongside the cars and other vehicles, trying to sell their papers. Olu bought three newspapers from a vendor who managed to keep pace with the car. This running transaction could take between ten and thirty seconds depending on how fast the traffic was moving. I glanced through one of the daily newspapers, which was similar to the British newspapers. I asked Olu how many newspapers were published in the country, and he indicated that there was only one national newspaper, and each of the twelve states had at least one. While I continued glancing through the newspaper, I noted that the majority of cars in Lagos were Volkswagens and Mercedes from Germany, Peugeots from France, and some Japanese models. There were only a few American cars, and they were usually from the U.S. Embassy. I was also struck by how many chauffeured cars existed.

Olu again noticed my bewilderment and explained, "We have a lot of ogas and madams in Nigeria. This is an unfortunate legacy left over from British colonization. They have servants for everything from cooking to driving."

We were now on Ikorodu Road, and what immediately caught my attention was the number of people not using the overhead pedestrian bridges to cross to the other side of the highway.

I asked if the government had considered building tunnels for the pedestrians, and he said, "Yes, they tried it, but the homeless and undesirables took them over."

Even with Olu's express service in the airport, we still found ourselves in the middle of the morning traffic. I made a comment about the bumper-to-bumper traffic, and Olu promptly corrected me by saying, "Traffic in Nigeria is known as *go-slow*."

While we were inching our way in the bumper-to-bumper go-slow, a distant siren sounded behind us. My first thought was of an emergency vehicle, but I was wrong. By the time the siren-blowing vehicle had maneuvered past us, I could see an army officer sitting in the backseat of his official dark green army Peugeot. The army officer's head was conspicuously buried in one of the many daily newspapers while his driver weaved in and out of lanes in an effort to beat the go-slow.

With a puzzled look, I asked Olu why the army vehicle used a siren, and with a puzzled answer he said, "The fact that the military is running the country, they can do anything they wanted to, and having sirens on their official cars is one of them."

Some of the motorists were trying to take advantage of the army vehicle's new path, but this inevitably led to accidents and more bottlenecks. Just when the army officer's vehicle was gaining distance from our car, we heard another siren from the rear. This time it was a Central Bank security van with an armed escort, and they were swerving from side to side, forcing cars to give way, also in an effort to avoid the go-slow and any possible attacks from armed robbers. Once again, other motorist tried following the security van's path with the same results. The petty traders moving among the cars during peak traffic periods compounded the traffic problem.

After crossing the Eko Bridge, one of the two bridges connected to Lagos Island, we passed the impressive civic center with high-rise office buildings punctuating the African morning skyline. I had to remind myself that I was still in Nigeria after this spectacular sight. Olu said we would be staying at the Eko Holiday Inn, which was the newest hotel in the country. The hotel was located on Victoria Island, an affluent residential area. Some of the homes in this area were magnificent and could be classified as mansions anywhere in the world, but they were all hidden behind concrete security walls in fear of their security. Prior to reaching our destination, Olu pointed out another large hotel called Federal Palace, which had been the pride of the country until the Holiday Inn was built. We entered a serene driveway lined with tropical plants, flowers, and manicured hedges leading to the new hotel. Again, I had to remind myself that I was not in San Francisco or New York!

The taxi stopped in front of the hotel where I could see an open reception area that led to the registration counter.

Uniformed hotel attendants rushed to our car, telling Olu, "Welcome back, Prof, welcome back."

Olu never said anything about being a professor, but I was not about to rain on his parade and decided not to question his academic title. We were now standing in front of the reception desk. To my surprise, the clerk was quick to say there were no vacancies. This prompted a serious discussion between Olu and the clerk that led to the intervention of the manager. After further discussions in English and Yoruba, we were given two rooms and treated as though we were the hotel's first guests.

I questioned Olu about using English with his traditional language, and he said, "There are some English words and numbers that are not in African traditional languages, and it's easier using English rather than trying to find a comparable traditional translation."

Jet lag was creeping up, but I was too excited to let it take hold. I enjoyed the view from my private balcony overlooking the hotel's swimming pool and a small fishing village in the distance. After unpacking, I decided to take a cool shower to help fight the urge to fall asleep. I had just finished putting on a warm-up suit when there was a knock on the door. A hotel steward asked if everything was okay, and after a quick visual check of the room, I told him it was satisfactory. He noticed that I was an American, and after seeing the sporting-goods samples on the sofa, he asked if I was going to start a company in Nigeria.

Starting a company in Nigeria had never entered my mind until now, but I was interested in his curiosity.

I encouraged him to say more, and he responded by saying, "My reason in asking if you were going to start a company is because I would like to work for you, and I believe that you will treat people fairly. I am an Ibo man from the eastern region, and in the past, our people felt so victimized by the northern-led federal government that we wanted to secede in 1967. To make matters worse, the country also has a quota system that favors the north because they were the least educated at the time of independence in 1960. When the civil war was over, the Gowon military government said 'no victors or vanquished,' but the situation has been to the contrary. This country has serious problems, and it seems like our leaders cannot solve them."

I had been in the country for only six hours, yet I had already experienced Nigeria's ethnic problem. This marked the beginning of my concerns for the country and its unfortunate social problems. The ringing of the phone interrupted my thoughts. It was Olu inviting me to have a buffet lunch in the hotel restaurant, which I accepted. The menu offered a variety of European and African dishes as well as a combination of the two. Olu suggested I try a dish called chicken *peri-peri* prepared in the African style, which was a spicy, roasted chicken over rice. To my delight, it was very tasty and became one of my favorite meals in the hotel.

As we were entering the elevator to return to our rooms, a voice called out, "Prof, Prof," and I could see a tall Nigerian about my age responding, "I'm coming," as the elevator door closed.

Olu said, "That's Yinka. I want you guys to meet because he will be helpful around the hotel." Olu asked me to follow him to his room, and moments later Yinka showed up. After introductions, Yinka told me that he was usually in the patio area if I needed him for anything and that he would check on me from time to time as well. I returned to my room and turned on the television, but there was no picture. I called reception to repair the malfunction, and they informed me that Nigerian television programming does not begin until 4:00 PM on weekdays and 8:00 AM weekends. At that time, the Lagos State government regionally operated one of the television stations while the federal government ran the national station. I was finally able to see Nigerian television, and the dramas intrigued me the most because they offered the norms and customs of the three major ethnic groups and some of the minorities.

After watching the evening news, Olu called and said he was ready to begin our evening visits with a few of his friends who lived in the local government of Ikoyi. This was another affluent residential area not far from Victoria Island. Ikoyi is known for being the former official residence of the British colonial powers. I decided to stay with the lightweight warm-up suit in efforts to advertise what I was selling. We spent about an hour at each residence, and the visits were friendly and inviting. The majority of the Nigerians we visited were either high-level civil servants, professionals, and successful business people.

As we headed back to the hotel, I could see people on the roadside buying late-night snacks. Eager to know what they were snacking on, I asked Olu. He began naming some of the snacks, which included *suya*, corn on the cob, plantain, and peanuts.

Olu thought it would be a good idea for me to see things for myself and said, "I think this would be a good opportunity to let you taste some of the snacks we eat in Nigeria."

He instructed the driver to pull over.

The first kiosk, no larger than a tollbooth, was selling everything from food items to mosquito spray. As we moved on, I took note of the Western-style dress, including the footwear, which were mostly sandals. The men were wearing either slacks or jeans with short-sleeve shirts or dashikis. The young women were also wearing jeans with Western blouses while the other women chose to wear traditional pullover dresses or wraparound skirts with matching blouses.

I brought the Western-fashion trend to Olu's attention, and he said, "It doesn't take long for the latest fashions to arrive in Nigeria. As you can see, the clothing styles come from United States and Europe. Tennis shoes are popular among the kids and young adults, and I hope we can get a piece of that market as there are no American companies supplying or manufacturing athletic tennis shoes in Nigeria."

Olu further explained that the majority of Nigerians living in the southern part of the country prefer wearing Western styles while the Nigerians living in the northern part of the country preferred wearing traditional clothing. He went on to say, "The reason for this is because the north was the last region to be a part of Nigeria and Lagos was the first."

We stopped at another small kiosk operated by a middle-aged woman. She was selling something that looked like a small brownish fruit, which was described as a kola nut.

After the seller rinsed off a couple of kola nuts, Olu bought one and broke away one of the three parts that make up the kola nut and offered apiece, saying, "These kola nuts resemble nothing you're familiar with back in the United States."

The taste was bitter at first, but it developed into a sweet aftertaste. He told me that this caffeine stimulant was used to fight fatigue and hunger. Additionally, it is used for curing stomach ulcers and diarrhea as well as in the manufacturing of soft drinks and dyes.

After tasting the multipurpose kola nut, I caught the scent of grilled meat, and Olu, who seemed to be always ahead of my question, asked if I would like to try some suya.

I asked Olu what is suya, and he said, "Suya is from the Hausa language up north, and it means grilled meat. The different types of meat are usually beef, ram, and *shaki*. And before you ask, shaki is the stomach of the goat."

I was tempted to try the shaki, but I decided to save this delicacy for later while Olu ordered the beef. Similar to a shish kabob, the meat was put on traditional skewers made from the straw of the useful palm tree and lightly seasoned with salt and cayenne pepper before being placed on the grill.

While we were waiting for the food to be prepared, I mentioned to Olu that the suya sellers were speaking a different language.

Olu replied, "They are speaking Hausa, and the majority of them are Moslems from the north."

This was my first indication that there were two major religions in Nigeria. After enjoying our suya, we started making our way back to the hotel. Olu pointed out an area called Bar Beach, which was within walking distance from the hotel. I would later learn that the beach was used for more than just recreational purposes.

When I returned to the hotel around midnight, I could see the guest had changed to a livelier set. I was not ready to turn in, so I told Olu I would be in the lobby and patio area for a while. At first, I thought the lively group was a roving party, with young women moving in and around the reception area with a carefree attitude. Being naive, I decided to join in the festivities. The club was alive with young women, and as I entered, three of the women gave me a suggestive look with an accompanying smile. Their smiles were tempting, but I continued into the club. I found an empty table, and while I was waiting for service, a young woman came by and suggestively asked if she could join me. Thinking this would be my first opportunity to talk with a young woman from Nigeria, I gave her a quick nod, and she began the conversation by saying in slightly broken English.

"How ya doing?"

"Not bad, and yourself?"

"You American?"

"Yes."

"You dash me?"

I had to ponder on this one, but I had an idea it had something to do with money. After letting her know that I did not understand *dash*, she confirmed my thoughts by saying, "*Dash* means tip," and I came back to reality.

After finding out that these young women were practicing one of the world's oldest professions, I discreetly declined her offer, headed for the room, and took a cold shower.

The next morning, I awoke to the friendly sounds of chirping birds and Nigerians traveling to their respective destinations. As I made my way down to the ground floor restaurant, I bumped into Yinka, who was on his way to see Olu, but when I told him where I was going, he decided to follow me to breakfast. As we were enjoying our meal, I noticed some of the hotel staff working on the outside of the restaurant chewing on a piece of wood about the size of an ice cream stick.

I asked Yinka, "What are they chewing on?"

"Oh, that's the African toothbrush. It's nothing more than a small branch taken from a small tree. You can also buy them from any local market."

As we continued our breakfast, I told Yinka about my experience from the previous night, and he jokingly asked if I enjoyed myself. While I was thinking of how to answer him, he went on to tell me that the young women were not only from Nigeria but also from neighboring countries.

I responded with a grin and said, "They were nice, but this was not the way I wanted to meet my first Nigerian or any other African young lady."

Yinka nodded his head in approval, and we dropped the subject.

I decided to take advantage of Yinka's presence and make a couple requests. The first one was for a couple of international phone calls, and he said he would have the hotel operator call me later that night. The second request was for the purchase of naira. Yinka said I could change some dollars where they sell arts and crafts in front of the hotel. This was the first indication that Nigeria had an underground economy, better known as the *black market*.

After breakfast, Yinka and I took a walk to where they sold arts and crafts and provided foreign exchange. It was a traditional rectangular hut that was modified to show only a thatched roof with no walls. I had a general idea of the exchange rate between the dollar and naira. Surprisingly at that time, the naira, which was artificially supported by oil, was worth more than the dollar ($1.40 = N1.00).

Upon entering the hut, I heard voices calling, "Oga, good morning, would you like to buy carvings?"

From another direction, "Oga, come buy from me. I will give you a better deal."

The ebony carvings were works of art, and I made a point to pick up some before leaving the country. Another voice reminded me of why I had come to the hut.

"Oga, you want buy U.S. dollars, British pounds, Swiss francs, French francs, or German marks?"

I told him I was looking for naira, and he was even more eager to make the exchange. Yinka told me that the majority of arts and crafts sellers are from the northern and midwestern part of the country while the majority of the foreign-exchange sellers are from the north. This was my introduction to the foreign exchange markets, and I would come to rely on the exchange rate not only between the U.S. dollar and naira but also against other foreign currencies.

I returned to pick up my room key and found a message from Olu requesting that I come to his room. I met Olu with two other Nigerian men; one was his cousin, who was discussing the upcoming birthday of Olu's father, and the other was a tailor who had just finished measuring Olu for a new traditional three-piece caftan suit.

I was introduced to Olu's relative, and Olu said, "I would like for you to join us this coming Saturday for my father's birthday."

I gladly accepted the invitation and, not wanting to intrude, started to leave. Olu wanted me to wait a few extra minutes for his tailor to measure me for a traditional suit. I was surprised and wondered about the cost, but Olu said it was a gift.

The next two days were uneventful, but Olu was busy moving around the hotel as though he was the head of state. Whenever he was in his room, he was constantly receiving awaiting visitors. Olu directed some of his visitors up to see the sporting-goods display, but nothing ever came of their inquiries. Olu felt the reason for the lack of orders might be a result of the military government's plans to place a ban on ordering all clothing items on or before October 1, 1978.

I felt Olu should have known something about this ban before our trip, and I told him that I was not prepared to wait in Nigeria to see if the government was going to place or not place a ban on an item that I was trying to import into the country. Olu agreed but said I should exercise more patience, but the thought of losing my sporting-goods business was becoming a disappointing reality. As I was leaving Olu's room, the tailor entered with a big package, and Olu asked me to hold on because my traditional suit was ready. The tailor handed me my suit and asked me to try it on. Instead of returning to my room, Olu asked me to use his bathroom in case the tailor had to make some adjustments. When I stepped out, they jokingly said I looked like a Yoruba chief. Olu said he was invited to a memorial service that evening, and he thought it would be an opportunity for me to wear my new suit.

I was tempted to decline the memorial service, but I decided to go because it provided me with an opportunity to experience another side of the Nigerian society. Olu had told me that Nigerians enjoyed a variety of social outings, from birthdays to memorial services, because they were a way to socialize. The services were already in progress when we arrived, and I noticed the street was blocked off for the ceremonies. Olu sensed my concern, and while we were waiting to be seated, he briefly told me that the city of Lagos did not have enough public or private facilities to accommodate the many large social gatherings. After several spiritual songs in English and Yoruba, the guests were provided with food, drinks, and religious music.

After my first Nigerian memorial service, we ran into some more go-slow on our way back to the hotel. Olu asked the driver why there was go-slow, and he indicated that it was a police checkpoint.

When we reached the front of the checkpoint, a police officer went directly to the owner's side of the car (right rear) and asked Olu, "Do you have anything in the boot (trunk)?"

Olu replied, "No, Officer, we are on our way to the Eko Holiday Inn hotel."

After a quick scan of the occupants, the police officer decided to let us pass. Still curious, I asked Olu about the police checkpoint; and he told me they were set up to stop armed robbers, car snatchers, and other criminals, but the check points ended up being more of a hindrance than anything else.

In the days that followed, the lull in business activities gave me time to mingle with the other hotel guests. It was during this time that I met a young African American couple working for the Johnson cosmetic company out of Chicago. We shared one or two meals together and would occasionally run into each other around the hotel. They told me that they had been working in Nigeria for over a year and that while there were plenty of opportunities for business, the country had some serious political, economical, and social problems. In their particular case, they were worried about their cosmetic products being reproduced illegally. Military rule and corruption were also major problems, but I would not become aware of these until my second and third trips to the country.

The following week, Olu called to say he had visitors in his room that he wanted me to meet. Thinking that they were business prospects, I hurried down and found two young women and a gentleman. Olu indicated that they were his friends, and he wanted them to see my sporting-goods samples. They told me that they were working for a French oil company not far from the hotel. Like Olu's other friends, they were impressed with the sample layout, but they were not very keen on making any purchases of sports equipment. I started having second thoughts about trying to sell sports equipment in a country that had other priorities.

As we were returning to Olu's room, one of the young women by the name of Pat said, "If you don't mind, I would like to check on you from time to time while you are in the country."

Thinking this would be a good opportunity to meet a nice young Nigerian lady, I encouraged her to do so.

Later that day, Olu called to say that I should be ready to discuss the sporting-goods business tomorrow evening as we were going to see a lieutenant colonel who was in the position to issue a purchase order for $250,000. The next evening, as Olu and I were coming off the elevator in the lobby, Olu noticed an American he had met the previous day. Olu introduced him as James Diaz, and although our meeting was brief, we would continue to see each other. James' ethnic background of African and Portuguese could be traced back to the Cape Verde Islands off the West Coast of Africa. We would eventually become good friends as we pursued our Nigerian business interests under Olu.

Olu indicated that since we were going to a military barracks, we needed to hire an unmarked taxi; the army did not allow commercial taxis on its property. As we made our way to discuss business with the lieutenant colonel, military guards at the main gate stopped us. After we were permitted to proceed, I asked Olu why military barracks were located in the middle of civilian communities.

"It was not intended that way in the beginning. The majority of the military barracks were there before the communities, and since that time the military never bothered relocating."

When we reached the lieutenant colonel's compound, we met another guard who asked us to wait outside until he informed the colonel. I could understand the extra security as the country had already gone through four military coups since 1965. After giving us the final approval to enter the house, a steward escorted us to a comfortable living room.

While I was admiring photographs on the wall, a young lady came into the living room wearing a blouse and a traditional wraparound skirt and with a beautiful smile said, "Good evening. Can I offer some refreshments? We have beer, mineral, or perhaps something hot?"

I was familiar with minerals (soda), but the word *hot* had me wondering, and I asked the young lady what was *hot*.

She replied, "Brandy, whiskey—"

And Olu interrupted, "Any liquor that burns your throat."

I decided to settle for a soda.

A few minutes later, the lieutenant colonel came out wearing a shirt and a traditional wraparound cloth that is normally worn around the house and compound. He wasted no time and said that he was authorized to spend up to $250,000 if we could provide him with a list of the sports equipment and a quote within five days. This was somewhat unusual as I was accustomed to quoting on items submitted to *me* instead of listing them to be quoted. Before I could respond, Olu said the quotation would be ready by Monday morning.

On the way back to the hotel, Olu provided me with a list of the popular sports played in Nigeria, which included soccer, table tennis, boxing, track and field, squash, cricket, tennis, and basketball. He also indicated that the quotation should be made out in pencil in case they wanted to make last-minute corrections.

The next day was Saturday, and it was time to attend Olu's father's birthday party, which was eighty miles away in the western city of Ibadan in Oyo state. I was anxious to make my first trip out of Lagos, and to my surprise James Diaz was going with us. Like me, James was an independent businessman who at that time was trying to sell video equipment to the state and federal television stations. I met Olu talking with James in the lobby, and moments later, we entered a hired taxi for the trip to Ibadan. Olu was wearing a traditional white caftan suit while James and I were casually dressed. Within a short while, we were on the expressway to Ibadan.

The stories I had heard about Nigerian roads and highways from the television and the daily newspapers were not too encouraging. The major problems were speeding, bad roads, car snatchers, and armed robbers. But what really caught my attention were the abandoned vehicles left on the side of the expressway. I asked Olu why there were so many accidents and why the abandoned vehicles were left on the side of the road.

He answered sadly, "The biggest reason is due to speeding, poor maintenance, and a lack of patience. We have no highway patrol like there is in the United States, and the national police are too busy fighting crime as well as setting up and manning checkpoints. As far as the abandoned vehicles and maintenance of the expressways are concerned, the federal government has always had the responsibility of maintaining them, but because of the lack of accountability and the inability to turn these abandoned vehicles into scrap metal, they remain on the side of the road."

As we eased our way into the capital city of Ibadan, Olu told us that the University of Ibadan, which was founded in 1948, is the oldest in Nigeria.

He went on to say, "Ibadan is known for producing cocoa, palm oil, cotton, timber, and other items. It's also the major transit point for goods traveling between the north and south."

Moments later, the driver came to a stop in front of a modest bungalow that Olu identified as his father's home. It didn't take long for relatives and friends to come out and greet the son of the celebrant and his foreign guests. We went inside to meet Olu's father. While we waited for him, Olu called for his young nephew Ade, who bashfully entered the living room with a grin on his face. Olu asked him to go and get two bottles of cold beer for his two American friends.

Ade appeared to be of grade-school age. I asked him if he liked school and what grade he was in; he said yes and that he was in primary six. As we thanked Ade for his services, Olu's father, who spoke very little English, emerged from his room to greet us. After introductions, he offered us a piece of ram's testicles, traditionally believed to improve a man's virility. After improving our virility through this traditional delicacy, Olu suggested we come outside, where we found a convenient empty table and continued our conversation as we waited for the festivities to start.

While watching the preparations for the party, we noticed movement in the back of the compound. It appeared they were still preparing food for the party, and I told James that I was going to stroll back and take a look. When I arrived, I could see women cleaning green vegetables and a man cutting meat.

As I was admiring their work, I said hello, and one of the ladies said, "What's up, man?"

The slang greeting caught me off guard, and before I knew it I was asking, "Are you from the U.S.?"

She replied, "No, I am from Nigeria, but I've been to the United States a couple of times. By the way, my name is Carole." As I was talking with Carole, Olu came to tell me that he wanted us to meet some new arrivals at the party.

An hour later, Carole made her way to the front and found us trying to get through our second round of beer, which is the equivalent to about three American beers.

Carole appeared to be in her late thirties, attractive, and a radiant personality. After introducing her to James, she said," I hope you don't mind, but I would like to know the latest happenings in America and what brought you guys to Nigeria."

For the next two hours, James and I took turns telling her of the latest events in America and our trip to Nigeria. She reciprocated by telling us of the problems of the country, "The British have put together something we may never recover from because with all the natural and human resources, we are headed backward instead of moving forward. There are at least three major ethnic groups and more than 250 minor ones [groups] in Nigeria, and it appears none of us can get along. I'm from one of the minority ethnic groups in Nigeria, located in the midwestern part of the country. The Ibo leadership was so fed up with the country that they tried to secede in 1967 but failed."

As James and I were enjoying Carole's informative conversation, she was notified that her transportation back to Lagos was ready to leave. Before she left, she promised to stop by the hotel. An hour later, Olu decided it was time for us to head back to Lagos as well.

We returned to the hotel late that afternoon and found the activities in full swing. I could see a group of young girls on the patio dancing to the beat of the drums.

Olu said, "Looks like we're in for a little treat this evening with the Sunshine Sisters here."

Upon asking more about the five talented acrobatic dancers, Olu informed us that their ages ranged from about eight years to teens. They were from the same family, and their father was their manager. While we were enjoying the young entertainment, I remembered Ade and the educational system in Nigeria. I brought the subject up with Olu.

He briefly answered, "Our system is basically the same as the British; the primary level is equal to elementary, secondary is equal to high school, and the universities are the same."

After explaining Nigeria's educational system, Olu said he was retiring to his room.

Before leaving, he said, "I would like for you guys to attend the Methodist church service with me tomorrow morning."

The request caught us off guard. I had to admit that attending a church service had never crossed my mind, and James felt the same way.

Nevertheless, we both said, "No problem."

James and I continued talking about the numerous business opportunities in Nigeria until the mosquitoes drove us back to our rooms.

The next morning, I started preparing for the services. I put on one of the two lightweight suits I had brought with me, but I was still uncomfortable. James, Olu, and I had agreed to meet in the lobby, and I could see James was also a little uncomfortable in his Western attire. Olu was cool in a starched white caftan as he waited for the hired taxi to take us to the church. The pastor was at the front door welcoming the worshipers for the Sunday service. We took our seats and began to enjoy our first church services in Nigeria. The service was similar to services I attended in the United States, including the pastor's customary call for visitors to stand and briefly identify yourself. The church congregation would have been comfortable in any church in the United States because the majority of the men and women were wearing the latest in Western attire. But it was the traditional attire that caught my attention, and I made a mental note to ask Olu about the colorful clothing after the service. Toward the end of service, the visitors were asked to stand and address the congregation. I spoke first, stating that we enjoyed not only the church service and the hospitality, but also the country in general. James echoed my sentiments and our responses were met with a chorus of amens. Shortly thereafter, we headed back to the hotel.

When we arrived, we let Olu know how much we enjoyed the church service and how nice the women and men looked in their traditional outfits.

He responded by saying, "Nigerians like to dress well, regardless of what they are wearing and even more so with traditional wear. Unlike in America and Europe, where women and men buy their clothes from shops and department stores, Nigerians have their clothes made by local tailors. Nigerian women can be seen in two types of dresses: the bubu, which is a one-size-fits-all pullover dress, or a blouse and wraparound skirt, usually with a traditional hat designed from thick cloth material. The men dress traditionally like I do or in Western suits like yourself, and for casual dress they wear dashikis and slacks."

Wanting to learn more about the Nigerian culture through the eyes of the inhabitants, I decided to have dinner delivered to my room and spend the rest of the day watching television. I was impressed with their television programs, which included children, youth, and adult programs. The foreign movies were from India, Britain, and America.

That afternoon, Yinka stopped by for a chat, and I assumed business was also slow for him. Yinka was an honest hustler, providing services to foreigners who were finding it difficult to navigate through Nigerian society. Yinka was like the majority of Nigerians who wanted to leave the country because of military rule and all the other social problems associated with their forced union. Yinka and I would share conversations ranging from military rule to life in the U.S. during my stay at the hotel.

I needed to exchange some U.S. dollars, and upon returning to my room, the phone rang. It was, the young lady I had met in Olu's room, wanting to know if she could drop by. Still wanting to know more about Nigerian women, I welcomed the visit. During the course of our lunch in my room, she indicated that she was an Urohobo, which is one of the minority groups in the midwestern part of the country. Pat was in her midtwenties, tall, and attractive. I noticed that she had three small cat whiskers painted on each side of her eyes.

I thought it was part of her makeup, and as I was commenting on her eyes, she said, "It's not makeup. They are tribal markings. I'd rather not have them, but my parents had them put on me when I was small."

"Do all ethnic groups in Nigeria have tribal markings?"

"Not all, but there are some who still believe in having their children marked at an early age as a traditional means of identification."

Pat said another unfortunate practice was female circumcision in which little girls are forced to undergo the ceremonial rites to keep them from having the urge for sex before marriage.

I asked if she had been circumcised, and she said, "Yes, but my circumcision has never suppressed my desires to be with the opposite sex, then or now . . ."

Her lunch break was ending, and I thanked her once again for revealing some of the customs of the Nigerian society. Pat was the first of my friendships and associations with Nigerian women.

James called a few hours after Pat left. He said that Carole and a friend were in his room and asked that I come down. When I arrived, they were having a joyful conversation about how we met. Carole introduced me to her friend Taiwo, and the young lady said hello in a British accent.

I asked if she was from Britain, and she replied, "Yes, I was born there, but I still consider myself a Nigerian."

I thought it might be a good idea to show them the sporting-goods samples, so I invited everyone to my room. Taiwo went directly to the tennis display and picked up one of the rackets. She made a couple of mock swings indicating she could make a decent return.

I asked if she could play, and she said, "There is only one way to find out; tennis, anyone?"

Even though my game was nowhere close to the quality of the equipment on display, I took up the challenge. She said we could play tomorrow evening at the Lagos Lawn Tennis Club, where she was a member. She said the club was originally set up by the British colonial administration for staff and other British citizens, but after independence in 1960, the Lagos State government took over the operation. There were other clubs around the city of Lagos that were started in the same manner, but today the majority of their members are Nigerians. Carole and Taiwo wanted to get an early start heading home because of armed robbers. Hearing this news made me feel a little uneasy even though I felt relatively safe in the hotel. James and I felt guilty keeping them any longer, so we escorted them down to the lobby and called for one of the waiting taxis.

Later that evening, Olu told me that we had lost the deal for $250,000 because the lieutenant colonel no longer had access to the funds. Olu's excuse sounded a little weak. Perhaps the lieutenant colonel did not feel comfortable working with him or me. Whatever the reason, I refused to let this major disappointment dampen my spirits. To keep my spirits up, I honored my tennis date with Taiwo that evening. I asked her to select one of the rackets on display, and after making her selection, we made our way down to the lobby. We approached a couple of hotel taxis, but their prices were too high. Taiwo felt we could get a better price from a taxi on the main road. While we were waiting for another taxi, a Lagos State bus appeared, and Taiwo, sensing a chance to save even more money, suggested we take it. The Lagos State bus was clean and efficient, and within a short while we were at our destination. The tennis complex was impressive, complete with a center court, stands, and about five side courts. I could have played a better game of tennis, but the thought of losing a contract for $250.000 did nothing to improve my game. After numerous attempts to keep the ball in play, I conceded that she was the better player. The shower facilities were not working at the time, and while we were putting our equipment away, I offered the racket as a gift, and she graciously accepted. Taiwo's residence was not far from the tennis club, and for safety and economic reasons, she decided it would be better if we took separate taxis to her residence and the hotel. It was only 9:30 PM, but the fear of armed robbers and other criminal elements gnawed on the psyche of the average Nigerian, and it was starting to get to me as well. This was another unfortunate concern for Nigerians, but living in the comfort and security of the country's best hotel, I felt relatively safe. This was the beginning of my relationship with Taiwo, and although she was pleasing to the eye, I knew we could only be friends.

Since there was no business, and it was Saturday morning, I decided to take a stroll alone along the beach in an effort to clear my thoughts. Upon reaching the lobby, I noticed a number of foreign male guests walking toward the beach with cameras and binoculars. The binoculars drew my attention, and as I passed one group, I overheard them talking about a Bar Beach Show. As we moved toward the main road leading to the beach, my curiosity got the best of me, and I asked one of the foreign guests if he knew anything about this Bar Beach Show.

As I struggled to keep pace, he said, "You haven't heard about the Bar Beach Show?"

"No, this is my first time."

"The government is going to hold a public execution for five convicted armed robbers on the beach."

I seriously considered returning to the hotel or at least going in the opposite direction, but before I knew it, I was caught up in the frenzy of the Bar Beach Show. While the people struggled to get a better view of this gruesome spectacle, a distant siren broke what had been a serene African Saturday morning. As the siren drew nearer, I wondered who was about to make their entrance. Within minutes, we saw a police truck carrying five wooden coffins, and as we solemnly watched the police place the coffins near the stakes, another siren rang out through the air, and I overheard some of the spectators saying it was the truck carrying army sharpshooters.

Religious members from the Christian and Moslem faiths were on hand to perform the last rites while a doctor was there to confirm their deaths. The only actors left were the "stars" of the show, and thirty minutes later a police prison van carrying the convicted armed robbers came to a halt. One by one, they stepped down from the van, with their heads down. The last man to step out made his grand entrance smiling and shaking his cuffed hands in the air. Like the others, his leg chains allowed him just enough movement to do a dead man's shuffle to the stake. The convicted armed robbers were immediately tied to the stakes without being blindfolded. They were given their last chance to repent according to their faith, but before the first volley was fired, one of the doomed men had trembled so much that his rope had come loose. The crowd became quiet, and for a moment an eerie silence overtook the Bar Beach Show. The policemen retied the trembling young man back to the stake, and like good character actors, the sharpshooters patiently waited for their human targets.

The first volley signaled the tragic end to this live drama, and fifteen minutes later, all but one of the condemned men had succumbed. This gave rise for some Nigerian spectators to say the remaining man had some kind of supernatural medicine, more popularly known as juju. Since I am not a believer in the supernatural, I felt it had to be that either the shooters were deliberately missing the vital areas, or they were poor marksmen. Again, bullets rang through the air, and after the volley we all thought that was the end. However, the last man managed to move his right hand to let the shooters know that their target was still alive. The military officer called for another volley, and once again, the condemned man found enough strength to kick his foot toward the shooters. Again the crowd called for more bullets. As the sharpshooters prepared for the next round, there was a feeling among the spectators and myself that in spite of the condemned man's supernatural medicine, this was going to be the final round. And sure enough, after the next volley, the crowd became silent as the doctor confirmed his death.

What had started out as a casual walk along the beach ended up being one of the most haunting experiences of my life. The crowd slowly started going their separate ways, and I sadly made my way back to the hotel.

I met Olu, who was on his way out, and he asked, "Have you been out for a walk?"

I told him I had just finished watching the Bar Beach Show, and he asked if I was okay. After assuring him that I was all right, he said we would have a talk when he returned.

With the execution still heavy on my mind, I returned to the room and tried to forget what I had just witnessed; but it only became more depressing. An hour later, Olu came by the room and again asked if I was okay. I reassured him that I was okay, but I wanted to know why Nigeria was having public executions. Olu began by providing me with a brief history of the country and concluded it with the public executions.

"Nigeria was brought together by the British in 1914, and gained it's independence in 1960. The country has only had one civilian government, and it was overthrown in 1966. The coup leaders were mainly Ibo officers from the east, and it was intended to be a revolutionary action. The north, however, viewed it as an ethnic coup. Major General Ironsi, who was also Ibo, became the first military head of state. The north was still bitter about losing two of its leaders, and six months later, there was a countercoup. This marked the beginning of Military rule in Nigeria. Lieutenant Colonel Gowon became Nigeria's second military head of state, and he would lead the federal government against the east in the civil war. It was under the Gowon regime that we had the civil war and the oil boom. Gowon would serve as the country's military head of state until 1975 when he was overthrown in a bloodless coup. General Murtala Mohammed became Nigeria's third military head of state, and unfortunately he would last only six months before he was assassinated in another coup attempt. But in that short amount of time, his military government established seven new states and gave the approval for a new federal capital called Abuja. The new capital, which is located in the middle of the country, would eventually take over from the city of Lagos, and this exercise was intended to ease the feelings of the north, which felt the present capital in the southern part of the country did not represent Nigeria. General Obasanjo took over from his military boss, and this brings us to where we are today. Now, with regard to what you saw this morning, before the civil war there was virtually no crime in Nigeria. We could move around at anytime of the night and not be harmed, but now it's not safe to move around late at night and sometimes during the day. It was after the civil war that Nigeria started witnessing armed robberies, and since that time the situation has only become worse. It will take some time before our military government realizes that public executions like the one you just saw are not going to stop crime in Lagos or anywhere else in Nigeria.

Olu's brief history of Nigeria and its public executions was disheartening, and to have it turned into a show was even worse. I thanked Olu for the information, but I was still feeling a sense of concern, and I decided to stay in my room for the remainder of the day. My thoughts drifted to the Bar Beach Show, the lost $250,000 contract, and the financial problems with the sporting-goods store. The thought of returning to the United States without any government contracts and witnessing the country's social and political problems should have been enough to keep me out of Nigeria, but for some reason, this unsuccessful business trip would be the first of many.

The remainder of the trip was uneventful until Olu invited me to a going-away party for the U.S. military attaché, Colonel Willie Haywood. The host of the party was a Nigerian colonel whom I refer to simply as the Colonel. Two days before leaving the country, I attended the party that was filled with merriment, African and American cuisine, and Nigerian music. I didn't think too much about the American and Nigerian colonels at that time, but they were destined to reappear in my journey of fortunes and misfortunes. The day before Nigeria's independence anniversary on October 1, 1978, I returned to the United States.

Chapter Two

Back Home

My relatives and friends were eager to know what it was like living in Nigeria, and even with my disappointments, I spoke well of the country. I told them that Nigeria was loaded with natural resources and business opportunities, but they were still trying to recover from a tragic civil war that led to military rule. I also told them about the variety of foods, the different ethnic groups, and last, but not least, the go-slow. I spoke very little of the Bar Beach Show, and when I did, it was only to nonfamily members.

Olu returned to the United States determined for us to make one more trip to Nigeria. I had my doubts, but my financial situation convinced me to make another trip. Thanks to a couple of good friends, I was able to come up with enough funds to pay for my round-trip ticket to Nigeria. Olu agreed to continue taking care of expenses, like hotel accommodations and transportation, which was risky. We also agreed that before returning to Nigeria, we should locate a company interested in expanding its markets in Nigeria. My brother and I agreed to give Olu and Nigeria another chance.

I would occasionally drive Olu to some of his business appointments, and while we were returning from one of his appointments in San Francisco, he indicated that he wanted to stop and see a young African American lady by the name of Lisa. Olu had never met Lisa, and I was surprised to see that she lived not far from my mother.

A young lady opened the door, and Olu said, "Lisa?"

The attractive tall young lady said her name was Linda and that Lisa was her older sister. While we were admiring Linda's beauty, Lisa, also a very attractive young lady, entered the living room. She appeared to be in her late twenties. After another round of introductions, Lisa and I briefly talked about our business experiences in Nigeria. But the majority of the time was spent discussing how Olu was going to assist her in importing a special brand of cosmetics designed for African women. Lisa's immediate problem was finding a Nigerian who could assist in getting a new cosmetic line into the Nigerian market. Before leaving, Olu said he would try to help. I asked Lisa and Linda if I could come back sometime, and they gave me an open invitation.

Anxious to talk to Lisa again, I dropped Olu off in Alameda and returned to her home. She felt more relaxed seeing me alone, so I started asking more questions regarding her business experiences in Nigeria.

She began by saying, "I had a rough time trying to do business there because the men didn't think I was serious enough, and the women didn't trust me."

Lisa only gave me half of the story, but I assumed that she naively became entangled in the web of failed promises and mistrust. It appeared her fortunes were a little worse than mine, but like me, she wanted to return if the opportunity presented itself. I became good friends with Lisa and Linda, but I would eventually lose contact with them after my second trip to Nigeria.

The sports equipment got me to Nigeria on the first trip, and we felt we should stay with it on the second trip. Attempts to save my sporting-goods store had failed, but I did find a sporting-goods company interested in the Nigerian market. In January of 1979, the Riddell sports equipment company and their regional sales manager agreed to meet with us in Olu's home. A couple of days prior to the meeting, Olu called and said James was in town on business and wanted to know if he could sit in on the Riddell meeting as an observer. I had no problem with James being an observer at the meeting, and I even thought he would add a fresh perspective to the negotiations.

I arrived at Olu's home two days later for the meeting with Olu, Mr. Grant, and James.

The company's sales representative arrived about twenty minutes later, and after introductions, Olu said, "We are interested in purchasing about three thousand pairs of assorted athletic shoes from your company. We would also like to know if your company would be interested in setting up a factory in Nigeria."

Olu had mentioned the possibility of setting up a sports-equipment factory, but I was not expecting him to include it with the shoe order.

Olu went on to say, "At present, there are only two major shoe companies in Nigeria, and they cannot meet the growing demand. Nigeria is a large market, and I know your product will sell once you have established your factory there."

The sales representative was not prepared to discuss setting up a factory and said he would pass the information on to his home office. After discussing the different types of shoes, colors and sizes, the sales representative wanted to know how Olu was going to pay for the shoes. Olu said he could pay by cashier's check or a letter of credit.

The sales representative had gathered enough information to start the order and said he would have a reply in two or three days. I waited until the sales representative left and asked Olu if he was sure he could pay for the shoes.

Olu confidently replied, "No problem."

Starting to feel uncomfortable with the catchphrase "no problem," I asked Olu to explain further.

"You see, even if I can't raise the money on this side, the buyers in Lagos will put up a letter of credit for the shoes, and I will in turn use their letter of credit as collateral to open up my own letter of credit."

It sounded okay, and it was agreed that Olu could handle the shoe order.

James was still in town two days later when we received a reply from Riddell's sales representative, inviting us to contact his headquarters as soon as possible. Olu placed a call to the company headquarters, and after speaking with the president and his general manager, they agreed that we would meet at their headquarters in Chicago in one week. The search for a company was now over, and not surprisingly, Olu requested that James travel with us to Chicago and then on to Stratford, Connecticut, before leaving for Nigeria.

A week later, we arrived in Chicago on a Sunday night, and apparently there was a mix-up with the accommodations because Riddell had not prepaid for the rooms. This was the first time I had seen Olu this upset. He was pouring out his frustration on the poor registration clerks. James and I were able to calm him down, but Olu made a point to recover the money from Riddell at the earliest opportunity. The next morning, the general manager from Riddell arrived, and before we could leave the lobby, Olu brought up the subject of the responsibility for our accommodations. While James and I watched in amazement, the general manager said it was no problem and that he could settle the issue in the office.

Upon arriving at the Riddell offices, we met the president and began discussions on the shoe order and the possibility of setting up a plant. Olu started off by asking the president for thirty days of credit on the shoes.

The president denied Olu's request, saying, "After we have completed one or two shoe orders, the possibility of a line of credit will be considered."

I felt Olu had an uphill task because the president said he could not commit to a factory until he made good on the shoe order. Olu, now sensing that the shoe order was in jeopardy, devoted his attention to convincing the president and his manager to make a trip to Nigeria to see things for themselves. Nothing was concluded in the morning session, so our meeting was carried over to lunch in one of Chicago's better restaurants. Olu was feeling much better now because Riddell had compensated him for the hotel expenses. After returning to the office, we agreed that the president and his general manager would travel to Lagos within the next three weeks. But before we left their headquarters and Chicago that afternoon, the president stressed that the shoe order had to be settled before any consideration could be given to the plant.

We met James's uncle at JFK airport in New York, and he drove us to the residence of an associate of his in Stratford, Connecticut. We were received by a young lady, and she graciously offered us a late-evening snack. The next morning, after enjoying a sumptuous breakfast, James's brother, who was introduced as Johnny Diaz, came by to say hello and extended an invitation for us to visit with his family as well. The extremely cold weather limited our movement the first day, but the following day James convinced us to brave the elements and visit the World Trade Center and some of the major landmarks of New York City.

That evening, after returning to Stratford, a shipping agent came by to see Olu and James about shipping two American cars to Nigeria. I assumed the cars had something to do with the discussions Olu had with James in Lagos and in Alameda. When the meeting was over, I asked if Cadillac Sevilles were the only cars they could find to send to Lagos.

Olu said, "Like the shoes, we have buyers for these cars, and they will be sold before they hit land."

I was unaware that Olu and James still had some unfinished business until the day we left the United States. Johnny came by that morning carrying a brown paper bag, and after greetings asked James, "Where do you want to count it?"

James said, "On the dinning room table."

Ten minutes later Olu came downstairs, and I could hear them counting and recounting money.

Twenty minutes passed, and James came out and said, "Would you like to come and help us out? We keep coming up with different numbers every time we count."

The last thing I wanted to do was help count money that I knew nothing about, so I declined the offer, and I am glad I did because this money would become a major problem between the Diaz brothers and Olu in the near future. They continued counting until, about an hour later, they came up with the correct amount. Johnny once again said good-bye and that he was looking forward to seeing us in Lagos in two weeks' time. That evening we left Stratford and headed for New York.

As we rode to JFK, I could tell that Olu was feeling confident about the proposed shoe order and factory deal with Riddell as well as the cars and cash money from the Diaz brothers. The six-hour flight to London was smooth, but the constant shifting of time zones was not helping my internal clock. We arrived in London that morning, but this time we left our luggage at the airport and proceeded to the heart of the city. I spent the morning going in and out of about four banks with Olu, exchanging dollars for British pounds. On the last exchange, Olu asked if I would exchange $5,000 into British pounds because he could not exchange any more on his passport. I was tempted to say no, but because the Diaz brothers were financially connected to this unknown deal, I agreed to make the exchange. I made a mental note of the exchanges, and if Olu was exchanging the same amount on the previous exchanges, the total amount could be at least $20,000 or more.

After moving around London all day, we arrived at the airport at 9:00 PM, and I was ready for the last leg of the journey. Unfortunately, our flight was delayed, and eventually canceled, until the following night. The airline provided us with bus transportation back to the heart of London and hotel accommodations for their disappointed passengers.

The next day was once again spent sightseeing and visiting more of Olu's friends. Later that night, we were finally able to leave on schedule. After arriving in Lagos, Olu once again eased us through immigration and custom formalities. This was my first time arriving in the country on the weekend, and it was a pleasure touring the major streets of Lagos without the go-slow. When the debate between Olu and the hotel reception staff was settled, we were once again given rooms. Olu was on the fourth floor while I was on the fifth, with a balcony overlooking the front of the hotel instead of the back. Later that day, Olu and I had a meeting in his room, and he once again assured me that the Riddell deal would go through because he already had a Nigerian board of directors waiting to form Riddell Nigeria Ltd. He went on to tell me that he had buyers for the shoes and would not have any problems this time around.

As I was leaving the room, Olu said, "Oh, by the way, I will be handling two other projects besides the one with Riddell."

This was no surprise because I knew he was working with the Diaz brothers and Bob Chang, but it did not stop me from wondering if Olu would have enough time to deal with Riddell. To keep my mind off this problem, I decided to give Pat a call to let her know that I was back in the country and invite her over for lunch. She accepted, and an hour later she was at the door. I had become accustomed to seeing Pat in Western clothing, so I was a little surprised to see her wearing a traditional bubu dress. The free-flowing pullover dress was highlighted with a matching piece of material tied around her head, and it made her even more pleasing to the eye. We decided to have lunch in the room, and, feeling comfortable about asking her questions, I asked how she felt about polygamy.

"Even though I am from a polygamous home, I do not approve of men having more than one wife."

She jokingly asked if I could marry more than one wife.

I told her, "If you were my wife, there would be no need to marry another woman." She smiled as I continued saying, "To me, polygamy is just another way for a man to legally have access to more than one female companion while young ladies like yourself are stigmatized for seeing more than one man."

I enjoyed talking to Pat, but the lunch break was ending, so we decided to continue the conversation another time. Pat would come by on several occasions, and we enjoyed each other's company, but unfortunately I would lose contact with her after my second trip.

Since my project was on hold, I had plenty of spare time. I spent the majority of this downtime in my room and occasionally went down to the restaurant or to the patio. That following Monday, Bob Chang and his associate, Arnoff Granville, arrived to complete the setup on the portable housing project. They were charged with energy and very confident that the Nigerian armed forces and other federal and state government agencies would purchase their portable housing units. Arnoff spoke with a slight French accent, and through our introductory conversations, he informed me that he was originally from Haiti and was now living in Berkeley, California. We became good friends and spent the weeks marveling at the opportunities that Olu had encountered and how he routinely let them slip away.

Bob and Arnoff's first assignment was to move the portable housing unit from its current site to an area not far from our hotel. This required cash, and it was obvious Olu was feeling some financial strain. He was spending more than $250 a day for accommodations, and the cost of moving the prototype was $2,000. Having nothing to do, I decided to tag along with Bob and Arnoff while they supervised the movement of the prototype. The unit resembled a freight container in its closed position; but when fully open it, could be used as living quarters, offices, or a classroom. This particular unit was designed as a classroom, and it came complete with everything from pencils to the national flag of Nigeria. Another benefit of the prototype was that it could be set up in one day with only a crew of four men. By the time Bob, Arnoff, and Olu had finished inspecting the prototype, it was too late to start moving it to the new site, so we headed back to the hotel.

Later that day, Bob asked how things were going with Riddell. I told him our meeting in Chicago went okay, but it was here in Lagos that I was having strong concerns that Olu may not be able to devote his full attention to all his projects. It was Bob who alerted me to my presently loose arrangement with Olu and Riddell. Until now, our arrangement had been based on a gentlemen's agreement, but Bob warned that it might not be safe to rely on Olu to protect my interest with the Riddell people because he represented the Nigerian side. He suggested that if I did not have an official agreement, I had better sign one before the Riddell president and general manager arrived in Lagos. The more I thought about the gentlemen's agreement, the more I became unsure of it. I wrote a letter to the president of Riddell two days later, asking him to protect my interest with a 10 percent commission for my participation in the deal.

The next day, Bob and Arnoff were finally able to move the prototype to its new site, which was located on the school grounds not far from the hotel, but they only succeeded in getting it partially set up. As a result, the roof was half open, leaving it vulnerable to rain, heat, and other elements. I expressed these concerns to them, but they said it wouldn't cause much damage because it would be set up by the following evening. Unfortunately, they spent the next three days trying to open the prototype without any success, and by then they had run out of money. Bob tried to get the extra working capital from Olu, but Olu felt that since the prototype was not open for display, he was not going to part with any more cash. With this in mind, Bob decided to return to San Francisco to pick up additional funds and to accompany the president of the prototype company back to Lagos. Arnoff was not too thrilled about Bob taking off for the United States and leaving him with an incomplete portable building.

As we were entering our third week in the hotel, the Diaz brothers arrived, eager to see a return on their investments. Later that day, they had a closed-door meeting with Olu; and when it was over, it was obvious to everyone that they were not satisfied with what he had to say. A day later, Johnny Diaz was more vocal in his disappointment. He made it known that Olu had taken money from them with nothing to show for it but excuses. The week was moving quickly, and before we knew it, the long-awaited Cadillac cars had arrived. Still having nothing to do, I went along with Olu and the Diaz brothers to Nigeria's new shipping port, Tin Can Island. When we reached this modern port, the captain of the ship refused to release the cars until the custom duties were paid. Three days later, Olu was able to come up with enough money to clear the cars but was still unable to find buyers.

Later that same night, Olu asked if I would let two Christian missionaries from Richmond, California, stay in my room for one night before returning to the United States. I had no problem with the arrangement, especially since Olu was paying for the rooms; and since it was only for one night, James volunteered to let me stay with him. The next morning, we all had breakfast together in the hotel's popular ground-level restaurant. The ministers once again thanked me for allowing them to use the room. They indicated that their two-week mission in the northern part of the country had been very successful, and they were looking forward to returning. These two African American missionaries were not only trying to spread the gospel in Nigeria, but they were also doing it in the heart of Moslem country. I spent the rest of the day loafing around the hotel, visiting with the ministers, the Diaz brothers, and Yinka.

A week after the Diaz brothers' arrival, Olu received confirmation that the president of Riddell and his general manager would be in Lagos the following week. The news of their pending arrival was welcome, considering what was happening with the other projects, and I put on a positive face in hopes of changing Olu's luck. When the Riddell people arrived a week later, I thought they would be staying with us, but Olu said that they would be staying in the neighboring city of Ikoyi, which was the private residence of a future Nigerian board member of the proposed Riddell Nigeria Ltd. My first thought was that Olu could not afford to pay for two additional rooms, which would have been ironic after he confronted the Riddell people about our accommodations in Chicago.

Unaware that the president had exposed my confidential letter to Olu, I objected to Riddell's accommodations and offered my room in exchange for theirs, but Olu said it would be difficult to change rooms at this time. Their rooms were first class in terms of service, but the house was from the turn of the century, and I felt guilty leaving the Riddell people there while we returned to the more comfortable hotel. Before leaving, Olu informed them that there would be a business dinner the next evening with the future Nigerian board of directors of the company.

I wasn't too concerned about receiving a reply from the president of Riddell before he arrived in Lagos, and I just assumed that the 10 percent commission request had been settled in Chicago. I was wrong. The next morning, Olu called and said he was having an emergency meeting in Johnny's room. I thought it was regarding the strategy we were going to use at the dinner meeting, but when I arrived, I met the Diaz brothers and Olu, and all eyes were on me. Arnoff was absent from the meeting because he was already on Olu's bad list as a result of the uncompleted prototype unit.

Olu started off by waving the letter I had sent to the president and stating, "The president of Riddell gave me this letter on our way from the airport yesterday. I took you in and treated you like my own brother, and this is how you treat me? Did you not receive your money on our first deal?"

While I was half listening to Olu, I wondered why Riddell's president would expose me in the manner he did, and I replied, "There was nothing in my letter that showed any betrayal of you or anyone else. I was simply trying to protect my interest, and unfortunately I waited until the last minute to do so. I was not trying to push anyone out of the deal as it appears the president of Riddell is trying to do with me. I also trusted you like a brother on the first deal, but we are not talking about a $500 order, and it was my fault for not getting anything in writing after the first deal. I am initially responsible for Riddell being here in the first place, so if I have touched on a sensitive nerve, you have my sincere apologies. I was only trying to get my normal broker's commission."

I was smoking mad at the Riddell president and felt there was no reason to hang around this so-called meeting.

James followed me out, and as we walked to the elevator, he said, "Hey, man, I think you were right in asking for a commission; and, like you said, you brought Riddell into the deal. Whatever the president was thinking, he should have at least responded to you before going to Olu with the letter."

I told James I appreciated his concern, and on that note, I decided to get some fresh air and take a walk along Bar Beach, where they no longer held public executions.

Upon reaching the lobby, I met Arnoff, who was on his way to inspect the portable housing site after the previous night's rain. I decided to walk along with him and air my views on the meeting with Olu and the Diaz brothers. Arnoff was not surprised at Olu's tactics of using the letter and including the Diaz brothers in the meeting because his business deals with them had failed.

He also felt the Riddell president was trying to knock me out of the deal by exposing the letter to Olu.

The conversation drifted to his situation when he said, "I had a lot of hope for this project in the beginning, but based on what's happening with our project and the others, I have lost all hope."

After the previous night's rain, I knew Arnoff would meet nothing but disappointment at the site. The partially opened roof had collapsed, and the floor was waterlogged, leaving the unit worthless. After the mournful inspection, we headed back to the hotel. We noticed the Diaz brothers sitting near the reception area. I thought this was a little strange because we would normally hang out around the patio area. I asked why they were sitting in the reception area, and James said he and his brother were locked out of their rooms. In an effort to make the Diaz brothers feel a little better, Arnoff and I offered our rooms to get them out of the lobby, but Arnoff suggested that since Olu was also responsible for our rooms, we should check to see if we were also locked out. Like the Diaz brothers we were also locked out. About two hours later, Olu showed up; somehow he had come up with enough cash to pay the manager of the hotel to let us reenter our rooms.

We tried to put this embarrassing incident behind us; and that evening, Olu, the Diaz brothers, and I attended the dinner meeting with Riddell and the proposed Nigerian board of directors that Olu was trying to form. I knew Olu's dislike for me was not quite as intense as Arnoff's, but the seating arrangement was a slap in the face. Johnny and I had to sit at a portable card table while Olu and James sat at the high table. James, obviously feeling uncomfortable about sitting where I should have been, looked my way with a questioning look. I pushed these negative thoughts aside and prepared myself to hear what Olu and the president had to say.

A Western-style meal was prepared for us as Olu opened the dinner meeting with introductions. I took note that the proposed board of directors was made up of influential people within the government and business community. The Riddell president made his presentation brief and to the point; once the shoe order was completed, they would proceed in setting up the factory. Some of the Nigerian directors were not aware of the shoe order and became suspicious that Olu was trying to pull a fast one. It was apparent that caution had replaced their previous optimism. The president also noticed during his two days in the country that all motorcyclists, except the police and the military, rode without crash helmets. He felt his company could modify their football helmets to produce crash helmets. The president also agreed to provide a general manager and a senior accountant at the insistence of his host, who felt more comfortable with foreigners in these positions than Nigerians. That was when I started to notice that Nigerians had a serious trust problem, and I began to suspect that the host did not have a lot of trust in Olu. Olu spoke again, saying that the proposed

Nigerian board of directors would live up to its end of the bargain, which included providing the basic facilities to operate the plant.

The president of Riddell made a surprising comment when he said, "Our company will honor its commitment to setting up the plant, but we will not be able to participate in the joint venture because our company is in the process of being sold. Our 40 percent of the joint venture is now available for any other foreign interest to take part."

The meeting was adjourned on that note, and as we made our way out to the awaiting vehicles, James approached me and said, "You understand what that means for us? We can pick up their 40 percent."

I should have been happy to hear this news, but after witnessing Olu's past performances, I had very little hope of receiving anything.

The next morning, I arose to what I thought would be an eventful day because Olu was going to show Riddell two proposed plant sites. After having a quick buffet-style breakfast, I met Olu in the lobby. He was discussing the trip with the two drivers who would be taking us to the sites. I quickly noticed that one of the two cars we would be riding in was a small Jeep. The Diaz brothers came down shortly after me, and Olu told us that we would be riding in the Jeep while he and the Riddell people would be in the Mercedes. It was obvious that Olu's financial burdens were starting to wear him down because he had never had a problem hiring cars for our transportation.

Our first site location was eighty miles away in Ibadan. The driver of the Jeep introduced himself as Douglas and said that he would try to make our journey as comfortable as possible. With that, we picked up the Riddell people and headed for Ibadan. Twenty minutes later, James and I were trying to find a comfortable position in the back of the small Jeep when suddenly we had a blowout. Douglas lost control for about five long seconds as the Jeep swerved from one side of the highway to the other. We were finally able to pull off to the side of the highway, and we thanked God for sparing our lives. Olu wanted Douglas to fix the flat as quickly as he could because the armed robbers were known for putting nails on the highway and robbing the occupants of disabled vehicles. After looking at the bald blown-out tire and the spare Douglas was using to replace it, my initial thought was that the armed robbers didn't even have to use nails to stop us. Douglas was able to fix the flat, and Olu said he would arrange for other transportation once we got to Ibadan. My only fear was that it would be another small Jeep with bad tires.

We reached Ibadan without any further incidents and proceeded to the proposed site. After all of the trouble we had getting to the site, we were disappointed by how small it was. We made our way to the local bus depot, which provided all forms of transportation from busses to station wagons. Olu thought it would be safer and more economical if he hired a station wagon to take us all back in one vehicle.

Unfortunately, the second site in Lagos was even smaller than the first one. The high hopes that Riddell and I had for a successful business venture with Olu had been reduced to nothing. As we dropped them off, the Riddell people indicated that they would have to start preparing to leave the country. As Olu and I made our way back to the hotel, the atmosphere was heavy with disappointment, and it prompted a silence between us that would last until the day I left the country.

Olu was already upset with Riddell for not letting him have a line of credit for the shoes and for stating that the shoe order would have to come before they would even talk about the manufacturing plant. The Riddell people, like the rest of us, had grown tired of Olu's empty promises, but before leaving the country they asked Olu if they could come to the hotel for a little recreation and a swim in the pool. Olu, feeling he had nothing to lose by letting them meet with me now, personally escorted them to the hotel the next morning and left us alone while he went out looking for another hot deal. I was able to talk with the president and his general manager, and I told the president that it was unfair the way he had revealed my request to Olu. He offered his apologies and said that it was a mistake on his part and that he would do all he could to keep me in the deal. I wanted to ask, "What deal?" but thought better of it. The general manager wanted to know if the shoe deal had a chance of going through. I told him that Olu had the ability to take the sweetness out of sugar, and the chances of the shoe deal being completed were slim to none. The general manager and the president decided it would be in their best interest to return to the United States on the next available flight.

The next day, Bob and his president arrived at the hotel with the hope of salvaging their investment from the crippled portable classroom unit. The president of the portable housing unit was attorney Bob Moran, and like the Riddell people, he had high hopes for the portable housing units, with promises from Olu that they would sell like hotcakes. The attorney took out his frustrations with Olu by running on Bar Beach every morning. Unfortunately, Moran could not run enough to elude his problems with Olu, and their portable housing project would end up failing like the other projects under his control.

While we were once again waiting for Olu to work his magic, he received an invitation from a Nigerian business group to visit the state of Benue, located in the central part of the country. The state is part of an agriculture zone that produces items like yam, *gari* (a food product made from cassava), rice, and a few other food staples. The Colonel, who gave the going-away party on my first trip, was also instrumental in the invitation. Arnoff declined the trip out of pure frustration, and I wasn't keen on making the trip myself because the same person that got us into our present situation was leading us there. But I ultimately decided to make the trip because it offered an opportunity of getting out of the hotel and see another part of Nigeria.

So everyone but Arnoff made the trip. It began with a forty-minute flight from Lagos to the capital city of Makurdi in Benue State. The second leg of the trip would be a fifty-mile drive to the Colonel's village.

After landing, we continued our journey by road. The fifty-mile trip took us by a number of small villages in the midst of a tropical forest before arriving in the Colonel's hometown. When we reached the compound, his family members came out to greet us with warm handshakes and hugs. In Otukpo, as in most other small rural towns, military and civil servants returned home from Lagos over the weekend to spend time with their families and friends. There were a number of small hotels in the town, but most of them were occupied. We eventually found rooms, but they were in different hotels. The Diaz brothers and Olu stayed in one while Bob and I shared a room in another. We spent the remainder of the day visiting relatives and friends of the Colonel.

That evening, we put away enough beers to help us fall asleep quite easily. The next morning, we had a breakfast of spicy scrambled eggs mixed with fresh tomatoes, onions, and canned corned beef. Later that morning, our host, a retired colonel, provided us with an excellent presentation for agriculture equipment, finances, and a possible joint venture with U.S. partners. But unfortunately, our group would not be a part of that joint venture because we were all having problems with our projects with Olu. After having lunch, which consisted of roasted chicken and beer, we were taken on a tour of suitable land sites available for large-scale agriculture. That evening, the wife of our host treated us to a buffet-style African farewell dinner, which included pepper soup for an appetizer and a main dish of vegetable soup, roasted chicken, fish, beef, and pounded yams. We finished off this outstanding meal with a tropical fruit salad. In our farewell speech, we told our hosts that we understood their needs and that we would seek out companies that could help in financing mechanized farming, storage facilities, and other allied services. With the exceptions of an excellent presentation and the unforgettable African hospitality, there was nothing positive to say about the trip. The farewell dinner lasted into the morning hours, and after getting a few hours of sleep, we began our return trip back to Lagos.

We drove back to the airport in the morning during those serene hours when the tropical mist gave way to the rising sun. We had an 11:00 AM flight, but when we arrived, the pilot could not start the engines and informed us that by the time the problem could be fixed, it would be too late to take off because of the Harmattan haze (hot, dry, and dusty wind) that blows from the Sahara once a year. To ease our discomfort, the airline provided transportation to the hotel for our overnight accommodations. The next morning we set out for the airport. This time the engines started, and we returned to Lagos.

A few days after we returned from our unproductive trip, we were boiling over with frustration from trying to do business with Olu. To lower the temperature, we decided that Johnny, Arnoff, and I should take the next available flight home. James and Bob would stay behind to see if they could salvage anything from their investment. While I was in my room contemplating my predicament, I received a phone call from the hotel receptionist requesting that I come down to the hotel lobby to see a visitor. I tried to convince the receptionist to send the visitor up, but then I heard a knock at the door. I was more curious to know who was behind the door than to know who was in the lobby, so I dropped the receiver to answer the door. It was Arnoff.

"I see operation lockout hasn't reached you," he joked.

"Not again."

"I think so."

The phone rang again; it was the persistent receptionist making the same request. I cut the conversation short and told Arnoff about the lobby visitor who refused to come to my room. Arnoff told me that it was a ploy to get me out of the room so they could double lock the door. Once again, the phone rang, but this time I decided to go down to save us from further humiliation. Arnoff and I slowly made our way to the patio where we met the rest of the lockouts. No one was much for conversation, so we waited in silence for Olu to work his magic once again. An hour later, he showed up with enough cash for the manager to once again let us back into our rooms.

Olu became scarce around the hotel after that incident, probably because he was embarrassed about getting us locked out of our rooms twice and losing three major business deals. On the day we were scheduled to leave Nigeria, Olu left word with James that we should leave our room keys with him. I decided to watch the evening news one last time before checking out. There was a report that Italy was having a national industrial strike that might affect our Alitalia flight. I spoke with Arnoff and Johnny about the strike, but they felt it would not interrupt our flight. Later that evening, we headed for the airport, and when we reached the check-in counter, we received word that our 11:45 PM flight had indeed been canceled as a result of the strike in Italy.

We had enough naira to take a taxi back to the hotel, and the driver sped through the night to avoid car snatchers and armed robbers. We arrived around 1:00 AM with the hope that James and Olu had not turned in our keys. The hotel had once again transformed into a livelier setting as the ladies of the night applied their trade. We found James sitting alone on the patio, appearing lost in thought. We interrupted James's solitude to explain what had just happened at the airport. Lucky for us, James still had our keys in his room because he had not seen Olu since we left. Frustrated and disappointed, we returned to our same rooms without Olu knowing. The next morning, I had barely finished dressing when there was a knock on the door. I was surprised to see not only Olu but also Bob, his president, Arnoff, and the Diaz brothers.

Unaware of his motives, I let them into the room, and Olu said, "Sorry about your canceled flight last night, but I hid $2,000 in your room last night after you left for the airport."

Olu had access to at least six rooms in the hotel, so I wondered why he would choose my room to hide money.

I responded by saying, "You did what?"

"I left the money under the mattress after you guys left last night."

I shook my head in disbelief as Olu continued to tell me about this mysterious $2,000 he had supposedly put in my room for safekeeping. When the money could not be found under the mattress or anywhere else in the room, Olu started blaming the hotel stewards in the immediate area. It was now obvious why Olu chose my room. Bob's president also picked up on the scam and said I was a victim of circumstances, and if I had traveled out of the country last night, I would have been accused of taking the money. With slumped shoulders, Olu left the room, his scam fully exposed.

That night, we were able to leave the country on Sabina Airlines, and during our return flight we spoke little of Olu. Again, this should have been enough to discourage the average business person to give up on Nigeria; but I still had this crazy urge to return to this wonderful but very troubling country. I also had the feeling that this would not be the last time I would see or hear from Olu.

Chapter Three

Nigeria on My Mind

Once again, I was returning home with nothing to show for my efforts but more financial problems; yet I could not keep Nigeria off my mind. Arnoff, on the other hand, had no intention of returning to Nigeria after his bitter experiences with Olu and indicated that he was going to reestablish his business contacts in South America. Bob returned a week later, and, as expected, he had gained nothing from his extended stay. James called a month later to see how we were doing and to inform us that he had met the same fate.

But before our conversation ended, he told me an interesting story, "You would not believe this, but a few days before leaving Nigeria I experienced the strangest coincidence. I was still recovering from my frustration with Olu and decided to hang out on the patio. While I was letting the tropical breeze drift through my thoughts, an Italian businessman asked if I wouldn't mind sharing the table. I had no objections. After introductions, he started telling me what had brought him to Lagos, and before he had said much of anything, I had a strong feeling he was talking about Olu. He said that his troubles began in Rome when a Nigerian associate came by his home looking for a cash loan of $5,000. The Nigerian told him that he had lost his money in Lagos, and he needed the loan for his trip to the United States regarding their business deal. The Italian said he didn't have that kind of money in his home, and it would be difficult trying to raise it because it was a weekend. However, the Nigerian was persistent and pleaded with the Italian to let him have whatever he could, and he promised to repay the loan when they met in two weeks in Lagos. The Italian was finally able to come up with about $2,000, and the Nigerian took off for the United States. Two weeks later, the Italian showed up at the hotel in Lagos expecting to meet the Nigerian to talk about their future business and to collect his payment. While he was registering for his room, he inquired if his associate was in the hotel. The registration clerk informed him that he had checked out two weeks ago and did not say when he was coming back. The Italian's hopes sank after hearing this disappointing news, and he realized he was not likely to get his money back. The conversation drew the attention of the duty manager to whom the Italian explained his situation. The manager then informed the Italian that his Nigerian associate had left instructions that the Italian was going to settle his hotel bill! The disappointments were becoming too much for the Italian, who had been scammed twice now. Fortunately, the hotel manager understood what the Italian had already been through and decided to drop the matter. I was tempted to tell the Italian what brought me to Lagos, but after hearing his story, I decided to drop the matter."

With the ending of James's interesting anecdote, we thought it was best to put Olu behind us for good. This was the last time I would hear from James or Arnoff.

During my two-year stay in the San Francisco Bay Area, I had several jobs: bookkeeper, warehouseman, and a few other odd jobs along the way. When I was not occupied with these activities, I usually found myself in Bob's architectural office. We were still finding it hard to believe that Olu could lose three major deals at the same time. While visiting with Bob and his wife, Carmen, who would on occasion serve as secretary, I met an African American draftsman who worked in the same building. During our conversations, I discovered that he had also been to Nigeria. Unlike me, he was there because of a social event called FESTAC (Festival of Arts and Culture). The Nigerian military government organized this event in 1977 when they invited Africans from inside and outside of the continent to gather and share cultures. I could tell he enjoyed his stay. It was conversations like these that kept Nigeria constantly on my mind.

In February of 1981, the opportunity to visit Nigeria once again presented itself. At the time I was holding down the office for Bob. Ten minutes after he had left for an appointment in San Francisco, the phone rang; and to my surprise, it was the Colonel offering his apologies for our misfortunes on the last two trips. The highlight of his call was when he said he couldn't make any promises, but things would be better the next time we came to Nigeria. He went on to say that he would be attending a two-month course in Monterey, California, and that he would call again in March. When Bob returned, I told him of the phone call. He also thought it was interesting and agreed that we should stay in touch with the Colonel.

In March, the Colonel called again to tell us that he was in Monterey and asked if we could visit him at a suitable time. The following weekend, Bob and I drove to Monterey, and the Colonel reiterated his concerns for our past experiences and his intentions to help us this time around. This was the first of a number of social visits during his two-month course; of the most memorable of which was a dinner in a senior citizen's apartment.

The dinner invitation came while I was working part-time as a bookkeeper, collecting rent for a senior citizen complex. I performed this task for about two months, and during that time I met two senior citizens I will never forget: Louise, an accomplished pianist and singer, and Margaret. They were both in their late sixties or early seventies, and on occasion Louise would invite me to her apartment to have a slice of cake and a short chat. On my first visit, I couldn't help but notice the piano in her small living room, and I asked if she played.

"I can play a little. What type of music do you like?"

"I like traditional, smooth and latin jazz, standards, rhythm and blues, and just about anything that sounds good to the ear."

She motioned for me to follow her to the piano, and for a few minutes she played a chord or two from several jazz tunes and a few standards. I enjoyed talking with Louise, and I would often find myself in her apartment to have a brief chat and listen to a short tune. It was during these visits that I came to know Margaret. I was fortunate to have the opportunity of meeting them both because they showed me the brighter side of being senior citizens. Their words of wisdom are still with me today, and I will always cherish their thoughts!

Prior to the end of my two-month employment with the complex, I told Louise about the Nigerian Colonel, who happened to like jazz. She was impressed and offered an invitation for him to have dinner and a little live entertainment that coming Saturday afternoon in her small apartment. It sounded good to me, and I said I would check with the Colonel regarding the invitation.

That evening I called the Colonel about the dinner invitation. He said it was too good to miss, and instead of me coming down to pick him up, he would take the bus to Oakland. I called Bob Chang to tell him about the invitation, but because of prior commitments, he would not be able to attend. I confirmed the dinner date with Louise and decided to relax until Saturday.

The Colonel arrived on Saturday afternoon, and we headed for Louise's apartment. Upon arrival, we found that another woman had joined our party. She was introduced as Mrs. Simpson, a cousin to Louise. She appeared to be in her midthirties, attractive, and possessing a self-assured gracefulness.

After introductions, she wasted no time in inquiring about Nigeria and asked the Colonel, "I understand your government is similar to ours?"

"Yes, we started using the U.S. system in 1979, and so far, so good, but our court system is still patterned after the British parliamentary system."

With a slight grin, Mrs. Simpson asked, "Do the lawyers and judges wear white wigs like they do in England?"

"I am personally against wearing any type of wig, especially in the tropics, but there are people in high places who feel we should cling onto the last vestiges of British colonialism."

"Didn't your country have a civil war about ten years ago?"

"That's true, we did have a civil war, and it's something we would all rather forget; but it has happened, and we're living with the consequences."

"How did it start?"

"At that time, Nigeria was made up of four regions: the north, east, west, and midwest. Unfortunately, the eastern region wanted to pull out of the federation."

"Why did the east want to secede?"

"The Ibo leadership felt they were being victimized because the north was blaming them for the first military coup in 1965."

"Is the situation any better now?"

"Yes, things have improved, but we still have a long way to go."

Mrs. Simpson, feeling it was time to change topics, shifted her conversation to Nigeria's current events.

"I understand Nigeria has oil?"

"Oil is just one of the natural resources our country is blessed with. We also have natural gas, coal, rubber, timber, cocoa, peanuts, and so on."

"Your country is loaded with natural resources!"

"Yes, and we are now trying to turn some of these natural resources into finished products instead of sending them abroad only to have them return as finished goods."

As we wined and dined our way through the afternoon, with an occasional song from Louise at the piano, I had several opportunities to chat with Mrs. Simpson. She started off by asking me how I got involved with Nigeria. I gave her a quick recap of my experiences without putting too much emphasis on Olu. In response, she said that she was a public relations officer for the telephone company and that her husband operated an entertainment and limousine service. I could see a use for public relations and entertainment skills in Nigeria, but I had my doubts about limousine services in a society where chauffeur-driven cars are a common sight.

As the evening ended, the Colonel extended an open invitation for the ladies to visit Nigeria, but Louise and Margaret graciously declined the offer, jokingly telling him that if he had asked fifteen years ago, they would have taken him up on it. Mrs. Simpson said she would consider the idea but wanted to talk it over with her husband first. She also offered the Colonel an invitation to a personal limousine tour of Monterey. This was a welcome surprise, and the Colonel immediately accepted the invitation. I was able to find accommodations for the Colonel in a nearby hotel, and before leaving he thanked me for a wonderful time and reaffirmed his belief that things would be better in Nigeria this time around. The next morning I picked up the Colonel for his return trip to Monterey.

The following weekend, Mrs. Simpson and her husband took the Colonel on a limousine tour of Monterey. That following Monday, she called to say that the Colonel enjoyed the limousine tour and that she and her husband were making plans to travel to Nigeria. I was surprised to learn of the Simpson's early decision to travel to Lagos, and I was looking forward to seeing them in Nigeria.

The Colonel had to return home in less than a month, which meant we had to complete our list of proposals to the Nigerian government. The list included sports equipment, portable housing, military boots, and blankets. Two weeks after returning to Nigeria, the Colonel called to inform me that the Nigerian army had accepted our proposal for sports equipment, military boots, and blankets; but the portable housing project needed further discussions. Thanks to Bob and his wife, we traveled to Nigeria two weeks later. The Simpsons said they would join us within a month. We left San Francisco around July 1, and after arriving in New York, we altered our journey by taking Pan Am's new direct flight to Africa. We had layovers in Dakar, Monrovia, and Accra before landing in Lagos.

We arrived at the impressive new international airport in Lagos. One of the Colonel's drivers met us at the gate and drove us to the Colonel's residence. Upon reaching the house, I noticed it was situated in a large compound with two bungalows for servants' quarters. The Colonel, his wife, children, and members of his extended family were on hand to greet us. The Colonel insisted that we have a beer before taking us to one of the many hotels, which had been privately built to cash in on the acute shortage of hotel accommodations in Lagos.

I was curious to know more about the extended family, and the Colonel said, "The extended family in Nigeria and other countries in Africa is similar to the welfare system you have in the United States. But instead of our government being able to provide these social services, our people are left to rely on the goodwill of family members and friends."

Changing the subject, the Colonel indicated that we had a good chance of receiving contracts for the sports equipment, blankets, boots, and possibly for the portable housing. This was good news, and we thanked him for his efforts. However, Bob and I realized that because he was a civil servant, he could not financially participate in the contracts. The Colonel stated that there was no reason to be concerned about him until after he retired from the army in less than a year.

Returning to our present situation, we informed the Colonel that with our budget, we preferred staying in one of the more economical hotels. With this in mind, the Colonel found a small hotel that evening, not far from his residence, and Bob and I agreed to share a double room. Unfortunately, the cramped quarters were far too small, and after expressing our concerns to the Colonel the next morning, he was able to find us another room at the Stadium Hotel, named for it's proximity to the country's national stadium. Before leaving us, the Colonel asked if we would have a problem taking public transportation to the ministry of defense on Monday. We assured him that we would have no problems.

The manager of the hotel approached us after we completed the registration forms and personally welcomed us to the hotel. He escorted us to our room on the second floor, which was not much larger than the room we had just left, but we decided to stay put because it was not going to get much better than this on our budget. The manager indicated that there were two other Americans staying in the hotel; this came as a welcome surprise. The manager also indicated that the restaurant was open, which reminded us that we had worked up an appetite in the process of relocating, so we decided to go down and see what was on the menu.

As Bob and I entered the small restaurant, we noticed several African Americans having lunch; and before Bob and I could sit down, one of them said, "You guys look like Americans to me! How are you guys doing? I'm Leon Coleman. I'm sure you know Lee Evans, and this is Thomas, our basketball trainer."

Meeting Lee Evans was another surprise because I had never met the former four-hundred-meter world-record holder. As we were shaking hands, Leon reminded us that he was a former world-class hurdler. He said they were in Nigeria to assist in the sporting programs, which were sponsored by the U.S. State Department and the Nigerian National Sports Commission. It was good to see these former world-class athletes passing on their knowledge to Nigerian athletes. They knew we were there on business and became even more interested when they learned that we were trying to sell sports equipment to the army. Lee Evans said that he was returning to his home base in the city of Ibadan. This reminded me of Olu and Riddell, but I refrained from making any comments.

As the men were leaving the restaurant, Leon called back to say we should try the roasted chicken. We decided to go with his recommendation for lunch, which was served with fresh sliced tomatoes, chips (french fries), and onions. We enjoyed the spicy meal, and it instantly became a favorite while at the hotel. Jet lag was once again creeping up on us, and after the meal, Bob decided to retreat to the room. I was forcing myself to stay awake in an effort to catch up to the time difference of eight hours, so I decided to take a stroll.

As I was leaving the restaurant, I ran into Leon, and he asked if I wanted to have a beer. This seemed like a good opportunity to fill each other in on the latest developments in the United States and Nigeria. Leon asked the waiter to bring two beers to his favorite spot, which was a second-story balcony near his room. As we waited for the waiter to arrive, Leon asked what brought us to Nigeria. I told him my story, and I was curious to know his. He stated that he and his colleagues started working for the U.S. State Department after retiring from competitive athletics. They chose this job because it offered them the opportunity to assist African nations and experience other cultures. Our conversation touched on the social, economic, and political situations in Nigeria. We both wondered why a country with so much to offer had made so very little progress. Our conversation was the first of many during my three weeks at the hotel.

The call for Muslim prayer from the loudspeakers broke the early-morning silence. Bob and I had a continental breakfast in the restaurant and prepared for our first trip to the ministry of defense.

We approached a taxi in front of the hotel, and I started off the bidding by saying, "How much to the ministry of defense?"

"Twenty naira."

"Too much."

"Fifteen."

"Four naira."

"Ten."

"Four."

We were working on a tight budget, so we made a motion to walk away, but the driver said, "Oga, come now."

We quickly entered the taxi and made our way to the ministry of defense. The driver took us to one of the tallest buildings in Lagos. I thought he had made a mistake and told him we were trying to get to the ministry of defense.

He said, "This is the ministry of defense."

After a closer look, we could see servicemen from the army, navy, and air force. Bob and I looked at each other in amazement and wondered why the military would locate their headquarters in a twenty-five-story building.

We paid the taxi driver and headed for the main gate, and after telling the guard which officer we wanted to see, he asked, "Are you both Americans?"

"Yes, we are both from the United States."

He gave us the once-over and said, "You are free to go, and perhaps you can take me to America one day."

Simultaneously Bob and I said, "No problem," and we made our way to the lobby of the towering structure called the Independence Building.

We met more security guards asking the same questions, and after another eyeball inspection we were waved through. The lobby was crowded with military personnel and visitors waiting in line to enter one of the three small elevators, which were long overdue for service.

As we were waiting, we heard one of the soldiers yell, "Attention!"

Everything came to a standstill; soldiers stood at rigid attention while civilians looked around, bewildered.

Being a former soldier, I stood at half attention and overheard someone saying in a low voice, "It's the chief of army staff."

The general and his staff moved quickly into an awaiting elevator, and the order of "at ease" allowed us to resume waiting to enter one of the elevators.

The Colonel's staff, having been informed of our visit, ushered us into a small reception room and told us the Colonel would be with us soon. A circulating fan in the corner of the room offered little comfort to the soldiers in their starched cotton uniforms. While we were waiting, the Colonel's staff introduced themselves. They ranged in rank from a private to a warrant officer. I could see the military was trying to set an example for all Nigerians by encouraging diversity; the Colonel himself exemplified this by having members of the three major ethnic groups on his staff. His personal assistant was Yoruba, from the west; the driver was Ibo, from the east; and his armed guard was Hausa, from the north. They were inquisitive and wanted to know what it was like living in the United States. We tried to answer as many questions as we could until we were informed that the Colonel was ready to see us.

We stepped into the Colonel's spacious air-conditioned office, and I was impressed with the furnishings. He offered us seats in the lounge area of the office and inquired about our comfort in the hotel. He then told us whom we were going to see regarding the sports equipment and the military supply items. He also said he had arranged for a fifteen-minute appointment with the chief of army staff. This was an added bonus, and our accomplishments on this trip had already overshadowed our dealings with Olu. The Colonel suggested we get started because our appointment with the chief of army staff was in two hours. The people and offices we had to visit were within two floors of the Colonel's office, and, unlike my last experience with Olu, the two supply directors had prepared a list of items and quantities they needed. We were able to meet the two officers and complete our appointments within one hour. The extra time allowed us to prepare for our meeting with the chief of army staff. We agreed that I would handle the sports equipment and blankets while Bob would handle the boots and the portable housing units. When our two hours had passed, the Colonel escorted us to the general's office, which was not intimidating but had a commanding atmosphere about it. This was surprising as the general's rank was the equivalent of a five-star U.S. general. The Colonel told the general that I had supplied the Nigerian Armed Forces basketball team with equipment in 1978. This went over well with the general because he had received good reports on the quality of our equipment and our prompt delivery times.

I assured the general that our equipment and delivery times would be just as good if not better than the last order. Bob showed the sample military boot and explained that the portable unit had multiple applications ranging from accommodations to offices, and the General said, "I like the unit. How much is it?"

"Sir, I'm sorry," Bob said, "but they are still working on the unit price in San Francisco."

"I understand, but can you give me an estimate?"

There was a slight pause, and I knew Bob was still working on the unit price, but I was also hoping he could at least come up with an estimate cost. The Colonel jumped into the conversation and asked Bob if he could give something in the range of an estimate cost. Again, Bob said there was nothing he could do until he received the cost of freight for a housing unit. On that note, our meeting came to an end.

We returned with the Colonel to his office.

He said, "I think you guys did well on your presentation of the sports equipment and the other orders, but I can't keep the chief interested in the portable housing project for too long."

While we were congratulating ourselves, the Colonel was informed that a young lady wanted to see him. Bob and I had decided to head back to the hotel, but the Colonel wanted us to wait until he finished with his visitor. The young lady, introduced as Gloria, moved with an air of authority and wore the latest Western fashions. Shortly after she and the Colonel began their conversation, a phone call informed the Colonel that his presence was required in another office.

The Colonel's absence gave us the opportunity to make conversation.

Gloria started off by saying, "Sorry for the interruption, but my name is Gloria, and I was wondering if you and your friend were in the country for the first time."

Without giving any details, I told her it was not our first time, and she responded by asking how we were enjoying the country. Thinking that this was not the time to bring up Nigeria's problems, I told her that we were enjoying the country and looked forward to seeing more of it. Delighted with our answer, she indicated that she was also in business and wanted to know if it was possible for us to discuss some items of interest. Before she could begin, the Colonel returned, and we decided this was a good time to take our leave.

As we were leaving, Gloria said, "Please, I would like to come by later this afternoon and finish our conversation if possible."

The Colonel gave a nod of approval, and I assured her that we would be available. At this time, I thought nothing of her interest or our business.

When we returned to the hotel, Bob said, "I think its time to break open that bottle of scotch whiskey I got from the duty-free shop."

I certainly had no objections because we had achieved more on our first day than we did in two trips with Olu. We decided to share our excitement and the bottle of scotch whiskey with our newfound American friends, so we headed for the restaurant. When we got there, Leon was the only one around to toast to our success, but the others joined in later. During our celebration, Gloria appeared. She wanted to know if we could continue our previous discussion in a more private atmosphere. I was still anxious to know more about the items of interest she had mentioned, and since Bob was feeling a little tipsy, he encouraged me to deal with the young lady alone. I suggested we continue our conversation in the room.

Back in the room, I offered her some refreshments. She politely declined and wasted no time getting to the point.

"I have friends who are interested in buying shipments of small arms and ammunition, and I would like to know if you can help me."

This request caught me by surprise. I told her that I do not deal in arms. Our conversation continued.

"You could make a lot of money selling arms in Nigeria."

"I know, but I don't know the first thing about selling arms, and who would I be selling to? Your friends in the government, armed robbers, or perhaps to your friends planning the next coup?"

I told her that it would be in our best interest to end the conversation, and she reluctantly agreed. As we walked to the door, she asked if I could keep our conversation confidential, and I assured her that I had no interest in spreading it around. When I returned to the dining room, everyone looked at me with surprise.

Bob jokingly said, "That was quick."

I told Bob what the attractive young lady wanted and how I turned down her request.

He nodded his head in approval and said, "I probably would have been even faster."

The next day, I mentioned my encounter with Gloria to the Colonel, and he said, "I apologize for her intrusion, but Gloria works for army intelligence, and it was probably just a routine check to see if we were dealing in illegal arms."

My brief encounter with army intelligence was a good omen because the next day the Nigerian army awarded a contract for the sports equipment and another one for military blankets and boots. Within one week, we had orders totaling about 1.2 million dollars. There was still a chance to sell the portable housing units, but the time required to complete the present transaction was going to take longer than we had anticipated. We decided that I would stay while Bob returned to Oakland to coordinate the supply of goods to Lagos. Two days later, Bob returned to California, but unfortunately, this was the last time I would see him.

A week later, the Colonel came by the hotel, and I was surprised to see with him Willie Haywood, the retired American colonel I met on my first trip in 1978. In our brief conversation, Willie said he and his wife were planning on spending a good portion of their retirement years in Nigeria. It was reassuring to see another African American trying to do business in Nigeria. Their visit was short, but Willie said he would stay in touch.

A week later, I informed the Colonel that I had enough funds to last one more week in the hotel. The following week, he suggested I move in with Douglas until the situation improved. I remembered Douglas from the last trip; he had driven the Jeep to Ibadan looking for a plant site for Riddell. That evening, I explained to Leon and the other Americans that I was moving to a private residence and that I would stay in touch. I had also met an interesting young lady while staying at the hotel. Her name was Maria, and she was from the West African country of Guinea Bissau, a former Portuguese colony. Maria spoke Portuguese, a little Italian, French, and English as she traveled through Southern Europe buying shoes and selling them in West Africa. It was through her that I met other West Africans from Gambia and Senegal, who, like herself, were trying to make a living from Nigeria's oil-rich economy. I lost contact with Maria in 1985, and like the other warm relationships I had with African women, I was fortunate to have met her.

Two days later, the Colonel came by to take me to my new residence. After saying my farewells and checking out of the hotel, we began our short journey to the little town called Ojota. As we traveled on the expressway, the Colonel informed me that the town of Ojota was not fully developed. They had no running water, and the roads leading to the main road were bad; therefore, I would not stay long. I was looking forward to the new move because it would allow me to stay in the country and observe another level of Nigerian society. We turned off the main highway and onto a small dirt road that resembled an obstacle course. The Colonel said the bad roads were a result of trucks carrying cargo containers and other heavy loads during the rainy season. Ojota gave new meaning to the phrase "town planning" because everything was done in reverse.

As we moved closer to our destination, I said to the Colonel, "I hope I'm not intruding on Douglas and his family."

"Oh no, Douglas is divorced and is living alone in his two-bedroom flat. He also travels every weekend to his hometown, and that will give you a little bit more privacy."

I certainly had no objections. We pulled into the compound, a two-story building divided into four flats, one of which Douglas occupied. Moments later, Douglas came out of his ground floor flat to greet us. Since we were already acquainted, there was no reason for the Colonel to wait around for introductions, and I assured him that I would have no problems staying with Douglas or with transportation. Douglas helped me with my luggage and gave me a quick tour of his flat.

As Douglas led me to my room, he said, "The bed is rather small, but there's a fan to keep you cool and to help with the mosquitoes."

I gave Douglas a nod of approval, and we moved on to the bathroom. I noticed buckets of water in the shower and toilet area, which reminded me that there was no running water.

Douglas looked at me and back at the buckets and said, "Do you know how to take a splash bath?"

I told him that I was familiar with splash baths, and I asked how he got his water.

"We buy it from the *mallams*."

"Who are the mallams?"

"They sell water for a living, and the majority of them are Hausas from the northern part of the country. They work mainly as manual laborers or security guards, and some even deal in foreign exchange on the black market. Their ethnic group runs the country."

With the exception of military rule, I was not aware of any political problems in Nigeria, so I held my comments on how the north was controlling the country. We moved on to the small kitchen, where I noticed a small refrigerator near the door and a kerosene stove by the window.

After touring the flat, we settled down in the living room. A young boy appeared at the front door.

Douglas said, "Shaboo, come, I want you to meet my friend Mr. Bob from the United States. He will be staying with me for a while, and if he needs anything, I want you to assist him. You understand?"

Shaboo nodded his head with a big grin and started kneeling to one knee in an effort to greet me and show respect. I wanted to spare the youngster from kneeling to the floor, but Douglas said it was part of their Yoruba tradition. Douglas informed me that Shaboo had come to buy food from one of the local *bukas* (restaurant), and he invited me to eat with him. I was more thirsty than hungry, but it would have been impolite to refuse food from my host, especially on the first visit, so I asked Douglas what he was ordering.

"I'm ordering meat, rice, and sauce."

"What kind of meat?"

"Beef."

"That sounds good. I'll take an order and a cold mineral (soda)."

Shaboo collected an empty 7-Up bottle and two plastic food containers and placed everything inside a plastic bag. I offered to pay for the food, but Douglas would have nothing of it. While we were waiting on Shaboo, Douglas told me more about the bukas. He said they are to Nigeria what fast-food restaurants are to the United States, but instead of hamburgers, these traditional restaurants offered what can best be described as home-style meals. Another notable difference was that the buyer provided the containers for the take-away food and had to have an empty container for each new bottle of soda or beer. The morning menu offered light foods like boiled eggs, bread, *puff puffs* (traditional donuts made from flour and sugar), *akara tea* (made from ground beans), cocoa, and coffee. Afternoon and evening menus typically offered one or two choices of meat, which were either beef or fish. The more upscale bukas offered a variety of menus that included beef, chicken, fish, goat, bush meat (any small wild animal), beans, rice, and a selection of soups that were usually accompanied with a side dish of *eba* (casava) or pounded yams.

Fifteen minutes later, Shaboo returned with the food, and before eating, we traditionally cleaned our hands at a portable washbasin that Shaboo provided. When we finished what I thought was a filling meal, we once again cleaned our hands in the portable sink as Douglas continued to tell me about the general situation in the area, "As you can see, the area is still being developed, and our present problems are the lack of public running water, an unreliable supply of electricity, and bad roads."

Douglas said the supply of electricity was so erratic that he was forced to buy a gas generator.

"There are a lot of reasons why things don't work in this country, but probably the major reason is corruption, and the reason for this is the lack of accountability. We have the people who can do the job, but when you are trying to survive in a corrupt environment, it leaves little room for improvement."

Douglas invited me outside to see his generator. He gave me a demonstration of how to cut off the main power switch and start the generator, but the fear of being shocked outweighed my need to have standby electricity. I thanked Douglas for the brief lessons, and we returned to the flat just as Shaboo had finished cleaning the food containers. Douglas thanked Shaboo for doing a good job, and in return Shaboo grinned and thanked him by kneeling on one knee.

As we continued our conversation, Douglas told me that he had been an unemployed electrical engineer when I had met him in 1979 and that he was now the owner of a building construction company with a backlog of jobs, a fleet of vehicles, and at least two homes. Before we retired for the night, Douglas informed me that he was leaving before daybreak and wanted to know if I would have any problems getting a taxi. I assured him that I would have no problem, and he started securing the flat by closing all of the windows and locking the inside iron security door. The flat, like other residences in Lagos, became a fortress at night to keep out the armed robbers. I thought it was unfortunate and unsettling that people had to live in fear of armed robbers and men of the underworld every night. This uneasy feeling stayed with me throughout my stay in Nigeria. It was only when I started writing this book that I realized the greatest assistance I could offer Nigerians was to constructively criticize their "unnecessary problems."

It was time to turn in, but before I could do that, a splash bath was in order. Over time I became a conservative user of water, but unlike the majority of Nigerians, who took cold showers, I preferred lukewarm water, especially at night and in the mornings. Douglas didn't have a hot water heater, so I asked if I could heat up some water on the kerosene stove. He advised me to use his electrical heating element because it was much faster, but if there was no electricity, I could use the stove as a backup. I ended up using the stove to heat water the majority of the time because of the lack of electricity and the fear of being electrocuted.

In an effort to drive off the mosquitoes, Douglas lit a mosquito coil and placed it inside my room. This was the first time I had slept with a mosquito coil, and the powerful scent from the smoke convinced me to buy a can of mosquito spray the next day.

Douglas told me, "Shaboo will be coming around after school to see if you would need anything and don't worry about giving him any money. I give him lunch money, and I also help pay for his school fees."

I felt comfortable with Shaboo's services, but I made a mental note to tip him as well. Douglas left me a set of keys to the flat. My first night in Ojota went smoothly, with one exception; at least two mosquitoes were able to survive Douglas's chemical smoke screen and found their mark.

The next morning, I took my splash bath and put on my new tropical attire: dashiki, slacks, and sandals. Being an African American, I had no problem blending in with the indigenous people as I walked to the main road. I made my way across the pedestrian crossover bridge that was designed to keep people from getting hit by speeding cars. I maneuvered through the hawkers and beggars who occupied the bridge, selling their goods and begging for alms, respectively.

From my vantage point on the bridge, I could see people struggling to get transportation, and I prepared to join in the mad rush. The majority of people were trying to board the buses known as *molues*. These vehicles were built on imported truck chassis and moved around town in unsafe conditions. Minivans were the next popular form of transportation, and their safety records were not much better. The best form of transportation was the taxi, and it was the most expensive.

I worked my way through the crowd of people struggling for transportation and approached a taxi driver.

Before I could tell him where I was going, he asked, "Where to?"

I told him to the MOD (ministry of defense), and upon hearing my American accent, he replied with an unreasonable price. Normally, I would bargain down the price, but I was not in the mood, especially after seeing the poor condition of his taxi. I quickly moved toward another taxi with the hope of finding a better price. His first price was within two bargaining cycles, and when he gave me his second price, I thought it was reasonable and hopped in. The driver noticed that I was an American, and as we motored our way to the heart of Lagos, he was keen to know what it was like to live in the United States. I told him that America is undoubtedly the most technologically advanced country in the world, but it has some serious social issues.

I gave a brief history of what it was like growing up as an African American and what led me to Nigeria. The driver said his name was Bayo, which is a popular Yoruba nickname, and he gave me a brief history of his life. Bayo was twenty-five, married with two children, and was trying to make a living driving a rented taxi while his wife sold food items. I encouraged him to say more and asked him about life in Nigeria.

"Everything is a struggle in Nigeria. In order to get accommodations, you have to pay a year in advance. We live in a one-room flat that has no running water, and we have to share the bathroom and kitchen with ten other families. I have children in public school, which should be free, but we have to pay for everything including school fees, uniforms, books, and even pencils. The political situation is no better with the military running the country the majority of the time. We have serious social problems, and it started when the British brought us together."

While Bayo was explaining what it was like living in Nigeria, it appeared we had encountered the usual go-slow.

Bayo said, "It's not the normal go-slow, and the reason for it is because of the body I passed by this morning. It's causing go-slow on this side because of rubbernecking motorists."

"Will the health authorities remove it?"

"As you can see, our social services are not what they should be. I've seen victims on other roads lie on the road for more than three days, but the authorities will try and remove him within the next few hours. It's a well-traveled road, and it's a source of embarrassment not only to Nigerians, but also to foreigners like yourself."

"It looks like a hit-and-run to me."

"It was probably by a hit-and-run driver, or perhaps a ritual killing."

"Ritual killing?"

"Yes, and the perpetrators tried to cover up their crime by dropping the victim on the road in the middle of the night to try to make it look like a hit-and-run accident."

It was bad enough knowing that a hit-and-run driver might have killed the victim, but to hear that killers used a hit-and-run ploy to hide their actions was even more disturbing. We finally reached the ministry of defense, but instead of letting Bayo go, I asked him to wait because I wanted to make some more stops.

While I was checking on my file, I was fortunate to meet a beautiful African woman who would eventually play a key role in my Nigerian experiences. I went to pick up a document from one of the offices, where it was not uncommon for some officers to have more than one visitor. The officer was engaged in a conversation with another contractor and at the same time talking to the beautiful young lady seated behind the contractor.

He interrupted his conversations and said, "I am Lieutenant Colonel Williams, and we are working on your file. Please have a seat next to that young lady, and I will be with you shortly."

As I came closer to the well-dressed and attractive young lady, who appeared to be in her late twenties, and we smiled at each other.

After a moment of silence she said, "Hi, I am Gladys, and my traditional name is Uloma."

I introduced myself, and I tried pronouncing her name without too much success. She repeated it, but this time phonetically.

"Ooh-lo-ma."

"Oh-lu-me, Ooh-lo-ma, Ooh-lo-ma."

"That's good."

"Thanks. And what does your name mean in English?"

"It stands for good home."

"Interesting."

She smiled and said, "It sounds like you're from the States?"

"Yes, but it's not my first trip to Nigeria. I was here in '78 and '79."

"I am from the eastern part of the country, but I have been schooling in London for the last four years, and I have decided to come back and try my hand with business and government contracts."

As a result of Nigeria's overinvolvement in the private sector, the federal, state, and local governments were the largest suppliers of business contracts. I admired her and other Nigerian women for their international business skills. Unfortunately, some of the female contractors were not given credit for their contractual skills because it was assumed they provided extra favors in exchange for government contracts. Our conversation was cut short when the officer's staff entered the office with my document. The officer thanked me for my patience, and after he handed me the document, I thanked him. Before leaving his office, I thanked Gladys for sharing her friendship with me.

She smiled and said, "It was no problem, and I hope to see you again."

Before heading back to Ojota, I decided to stop by the Nigerian Telecommunications (NITEL) office and give Bob a call. This government-owned company was trying to keep up with the demands for individual phone line services in Nigeria, but they were unable to do so. In an effort to reduce the request for national and international phone services, they established public NITEL offices throughout the city of Lagos and other major cities in the country. Their phone booths were similar to the ones in United States, and some were located on public streets while others were inside NITEL offices.

During our conversation, Bob said that the manufacturer was no longer interested in the portable units. From the tone of Bob's voice, I could tell he was not going to pursue the portable housing project, so I shifted the conversation to the projects at hand. Bob said he would contact Mr. Grant regarding the sports equipment and line up the banking facilities to handle the letters of credit.

On my way back to Ojota, I asked Bayo to stop by the Stadium Hotel for a quick visit with Leon and his colleagues. Leon said they were making plans to return to the United States because of the administration problems with the Nigerian sports administrator. What started out as a promising program for Nigerian athletes and their U.S instructors had ended up being a wasted opportunity. My visit ended on a sour note, and all I could do was wish them well. As we continued our journey to Ojota, I considered the benefits of having a driver at my disposal, so I asked Bayo if I could hire him on a daily basis. He agreed, and I never had to worry about transportation throughout my stay in Ojota.

Time passed quickly in Ojota, and a month later, the contract that called for my deposit to be paid in local currency was approved. I was going to miss Douglas and Shaboo as well as the other people I had the opportunity of meeting while I was there. Before leaving, I offered to compensate Douglas for allowing me to stay with him, but again, he would have nothing of it. With that, I headed for my new accommodations in the Palace Hotel, which was located in the local government area of Ikeja.

Before relating my experience of getting a file through the Nigerian government, I should explain how government contracts and financial documents were processed at that time. My contract had to go through three major steps involving several departments. The first step was through the ministry of defense, the second step was the ministry of finance, and the third and final step was with the Central Bank. My file was ready to leave the ministry of defense, and I was able to get it through without any major delays or bribes. I was hoping for the same success with the ministry of finance, where all contracts requiring foreign exchange had to be processed. The ministry of finance is located in Ikoyi, and after reaching the first department, the finance officer said that my original invoice was missing from my file.

"What do you mean my invoice is missing?"

He looked at me and said, "It's possible that a clerk misplaced it, or perhaps a messenger could have lost it while transporting your file from the ministry of defense to our ministry. Whatever the case, the longer your incomplete file sits on my desk, the longer it will take to pass it on."

I told him that I was on a business visa, and my time was running short.

He replied, "If you wish, I could return your file to the ministry of defense, and you could start the process all over again, but I think it would be in your best interest to make a decision soon."

I had a strong suspicion that he wanted a bribe, but all of this was new to me, so I told him I would return in the morning. That evening I met with the Colonel, and after explaining my recent experiences with the finance officer, he suggested that it would probably be faster if I took some money with me and asked Sergeant Rivers, the army supply clerk from the sports camp, to accompany me. I had become friendly with the sergeant, so I contacted him the following day, and he agreed to come with me in civilian clothes in an effort to ease the stress of negotiating my first bribe the following morning.

The next morning, I picked up the sergeant and headed for the ministry of finance. After pleasantries and the reassurance that my newfound friend was not a member of the security service, the finance officer agreed to reopen the unofficial negotiations. It sounded unreal, and after the finance officer finished explaining the situation, the sergeant discreetly tapped me on the leg and I asked the finance officer if we could be excused for a moment.

After walking a safe distance from his office, the sergeant said, "Your original invoice is with this guy, and all he wants is some money before passing the file on." I needed to get the file moving, so I asked the sergeant to see how much he wanted while I waited outside. He returned a few minutes later and said that the officer was looking for three thousand naira, which was about the same in U.S. dollars at that time. I returned with the sergeant, and I was able to bring down the price to one thousand naira. The finance officer said he had to check with his boss for his approval.

He left the office with my file, and the sergeant said, "It's a good chance he will not see his boss. He's probably in some room inserting your original invoice."

When he returned, the finance officer smiled broadly as he informed me that my invoice had miraculously found its way back into the file. After verifying that the original invoice was in my file, I gave the finance officer one thousand naira, and he said, "Sorry for the inconvenience, but sometimes in Nigeria, it's faster to take the express road rather than start all over again."

That evening, I told the Colonel the file was once again on the move and mentioned my concerns about the possibility of running into another incident like the one with the finance officer.

The Colonel said, "It's unfortunate that this crazy practice is so deeply rooted in our society. It all started with the financial windfall from oil in the '70s. And it's going to take a complete overhaul of the system to bring the leaders and the people back to their senses."

The next day, one of the Colonel's staff came by my room to tell me that I had an important message at the Colonel's house and that his wife would give it to me. I went to the Colonel's house, and his wife, who was normally in a cheerful mood, had a concerned look on her face.

She told me, "I am sorry, but Bob Chang's wife called last night and said he died two days ago from a heart attack."

I was at a loss for words for this unwelcome surprise, and it was unfortunate that Bob had come so close to completing his first deal in Nigeria, and it had to end like this.

The Colonel's wife asked if I was okay. I assured her that I was all right, and as I was thanking her for the unfortunate news, the Colonel arrived. After expressing his condolences, he said that it would be better if I stayed back and sent our concerns through a cablegram. For the next two days, I wondered who was going to take Bob's place. I wanted Mr. Grant, but his schedule would not allow him to participate fully because he was teaching, coaching, and operating his own business; and asking Bob's wife was out of the question. I finally came up with an attorney by the name of Bruce Kwan, whom I had met through another mutual friend in 1982. He said he could take over for Bob and assured me that Mr. Grant would be kept on as a consultant.

The Colonel informed me that the Simpsons were in the country and that they were staying at a nearby hotel. That evening I visited them, and I was surprised to hear that after being in the country for one week, they were already working for a Nigerian businessman, operating his new nightclub called the Lord's. I could see they were more than satisfied with their foreign employment because they were all smiles.

Mrs. Simpson said, "I know you were expecting us to be doing business similar to yours, but we're getting paid well, and we have all the perks to go along with our new executive positions. We even have the owner's permission to hire another American as the club manager, and he will be here in two weeks. As you can see, we are living in the hotel's executive suite until they can find us a duplex at the owner's expense. We have a chauffeur-driven car, and our meals are prepared by a French-trained chef."

I was happy for the Simpsons, but I found it strange that they tied themselves down so quickly before exploring other business opportunities in the country; however, it was their choice, and I decided to offer them my support.

Most Saturdays I would visit with the Colonel and his family. On one particular Saturday, the Colonel let one of his drivers take me back to the hotel. This time we had some extra company with two of the Colonel's children and his future daughter-in-law. The Colonel's family knew that I was looking for accommodations, and his daughter-in-law suggested I meet a friend of hers by the name of Ada, whom she thought could be helpful in finding a flat.

"How do you pronounce her name?" I asked.

"Ah-da."

"Ada, Ada."

"That's good, but before we get there, I want you to know a little bit about her. She's single, in her late twenties or early thirties, and known as a wheeler-dealer type. She owns a beauty salon and a clothing boutique store, and since you are a bachelor businessman, I thought it might not be a bad idea for you two to know each other."

"I see."

"I would like for you to meet her."

"I wouldn't mind."

We stopped by Ada's beauty salon, which was not far from the hotel, and after brief introductions, my first impression of this small fiery young lady was that she was everything the daughter-in-law said she was. Ada represented a new generation of retail businesses in Nigeria, and she was doing it as a single woman. Her beauty salon provided not only traditional hairstyle, but also the latest African American hairstyles. The driver was waiting for us to resume our journey, but before leaving, I gave her my address.

The next afternoon, I was pleasantly surprised when she came by the hotel.

"Would you like to go for a ride?" she asked.

I had nothing planned, so I welcomed the opportunity. We rode in her vintage white Peugeot as she demonstrated how to get around town while avoiding obstacles.

Some of the moves she made were illegal, but she would say, "You have to drive like this; otherwise it will take forever."

Ada said one of the tricks to driving in Lagos is knowing the alternate routes in case you ran into go-slow or checkpoints, which was more often than not. I took note of her driving tips and made a point to use some of them in the future. Later that evening, she dropped me off at the hotel with a promise to stay in touch. This marked the beginning of my noncommittal relationship with Ada.

The next day, I called the attorney, and he gave me another mild shock when he informed me that the bank was not accepting the three letters of credit. I was under the impression that an irrevocable letter of credit was as good as or better than cash, but this was not so. The Bank of America would not accept our letters of credit because our company was less than a year old, and there was a high number of international fraud cases that originated from Nigeria. Contracts worth more than a million dollars were now in jeopardy.

I now had three useless letters of credit, and the only option left was to get the army to pay by check. I explained the problem to the Colonel, and he said he would discuss it with the payment department. Two days later, the Colonel said the army was trying to make arrangements to pay for the sports equipment through their Nigerian embassy in Washington DC, but the other two contracts would have to be honored by the banks, subcontracted, or forgotten. It was going to be difficult trying to overcome this business setback because getting new contracts would be much harder. It was not a complete loss, but it was still hard to concede that I had lost the majority of the contracts. I called the attorney to explain the situation, and a week later he picked up a partial payment check from the Nigerian embassy in Washington DC. I decided to stay in Lagos and take receipt of the goods.

The Colonel was close to retirement, and in preparation, he moved his family to his hometown. This left him with an empty, five-bedroom house for the next two months. He suggested that I stay there until his occupancy ended. A break from hotel life was welcome news, and I wasted no time in moving the next day.

That following weekend, the Colonel and I traveled to his hometown to witness the coming-out ceremony for a chief who had been fasting and praying for thirty days. The chief's son, who was another high-ranking civil servant, was going to be our host, and I was intrigued by the invitation. We took a midmorning flight to the eastern city of Enugu and then drove the remainder of the journey. As the Colonel was bargaining for our road transportation, he met two of his young kinsmen. They were headed in the same direction and offered to give us a lift. The Colonel and I took our seats in the back while the driver and his friend began our journey to the Colonel's hometown. The journey started off fine, but soon after we got on the highway, all caution was thrown to the wind. I noticed the driver was not wearing any visible charms, but I had to assume he had charm insurance. We were on a two-lane highway, playing a deadly game of "pass everything in front of you without getting hit by oncoming traffic." The Colonel cautioned him to slow down a couple of times, but as soon as he dozed off, the young driver left no room between his gas foot and the floorboard. It was with a sigh of relief and some disbelief that we reached our destination alive.

The Colonel's family was happy to see us. After a round of greetings, the Colonel gave me a tour of his property, which was three times the size of his compound in Lagos. An hour later, we were eating pepper soup and drinking bottles of cold beer in one of the local restaurants. We repeated this process in another restaurant, with one or two visits in between, and after consuming several bottles of beer by nightfall, I was ready to rest. The Colonel checked me into a hotel not far from the compound, and I had no problems falling asleep. I was awakened the next morning by a knock on the hotel door. It was one of the Colonel's children informing me that they were ready to leave for the coming-out ceremonies.

After a quick breakfast, we rode about twenty-five miles to the village. Upon our arrival, we enjoyed another round of greetings as the village welcomed the chief's son and his guest to his father's ceremonies. I could hear drums in the distance, and then a momentary pause, followed by the sound of drums coming from the Chief's son village. The chief's son indicated that the drummers from this particular village and the surrounding ones were sending and receiving messages announcing that the head chief was about to emerge. As we took our seats, I noticed a small house set behind a couple of small trees. The house was made from imported cement instead of clay, but it did have a thatched roof like the other structures in the village. I continued to absorb the rural village life while we were provided with two pans of water, a bar of soap, and a towel. The Colonel said they had prepared lunch for us; our meal consisted of vegetable soup made from greens similar to spinach and a questionable food item called bush meat. As stated earlier, bush meat could be any one of a variety of small wild animals; and this being my first time eating it, I asked what type of meat it was.

With a slight grin, the Colonel said, "The bush meat we are eating is called a grass cutter. It's about the size of a rabbit, and it eats like a rabbit, but it's in the rat family."

At first, I had a problem with eating any kind of rodent, but after my first couple bites of this smoked grass cutter, it became one of my favorite meats. I was a little clumsy eating with my fingers at first, but I quickly caught on by watching others. While we were eating, I watched one of the young villagers climb a palm tree with a rope around his waist and a special calabash gourd (a container for carrying liquids and other items). He extracted a special liquid called palm wine from the top of the palm tree. He came down slowly in an effort to protect this intoxicating liquid, and I was presented with a glass. It looked like watered-down milk, and had a tangy taste that was actually cool and soothing to the throat.

The time was nearing for the chief to emerge from his solitude of fasting and prayer. Our host said, under their tradition, the Colonel and I were not allowed to be the first ones to see the chief emerge, and we were promptly given a tour of the village. As we made our way through the village, our host pointed out some of the key areas. These included the market, the living quarters, and the assembly grounds where the festivities were being held. As our host escorted us through the major parts of the village, I could see the other traditional dwellings that were made from clay with the familiar thatched roof. We came to a clearing, and I could see an outdoor platform where the chief was dressed in his finest clothes and sitting proudly on his throne. It was from this area that the chief would officially greet those who had come to pay homage to his kingdom. I observed that the chief's eyes were not fixed on any one thing, yet he was aware of the people staring at him. I watched other chiefs and dignitaries pay their respects to the head chief until his son said it was now my turn to pay homage. Not knowing what to do, I asked my host how I should greet the chief. He said their tradition would not allow the chief to make direct eye contact with me, but I was permitted to look at him. He also said there was no handshaking, and all I had to do was nod my head in approval after being introduced. The remainder of day was filled with merriment, food, and drink that were freshly prepared that morning. The entertainment consisted of colorful masquerades and other acts, including a high-stepping dance where the objective was to run as fast as you could while standing in one spot. I enjoyed this historic outing, and after thanking the host for his enlightening entertainment, we returned to the Colonel's home town. That following morning we returned to Lagos.

My first task upon returning to Lagos was to buy a car and find private accommodations. That following weekend, the Colonel drove me to the Peugeot assembly plant in the city of Ibadan. It took less than one hour to conduct our business, and after paying for the 504 Peugeot, my transportation problems were temporarily over. The process for obtaining a driver's license was similar to that in the United States. With the help of Ada, I was able to get my driving license and find a three-bedroom flat in the local government area of Ikeja. I purchased furniture, which was manufactured locally, and an imported stove, refrigerator, television, and stereo from the major department stores and the popular Alaba market. Alaba is similar to the other markets in Lagos, but the majority of their items are imported.

One of the major problems I had with the flat was the lack of running water. Living on the third floor only compounded the problem. I was able to solve this difficulty by hiring one of the Colonel's former cooks, who also worked as a servant. I purchased well water from water tankers and the mallams, and I treated it by boiling it and running it through a portable water filter. The untreated water was used for bathing and other chores around the flat. Having constant electricity in Lagos was difficult in itself, but in our particular area, it was only at half voltage when it was available at all. This inconvenience put all electrical appliances at serious risk, and to make matters worse, the electrical company would sometimes surprise the residence with a surge of electrical power, causing even more damage.

The government-owned company responsible for the irregular supply of electricity was the National Electric Power Authority. A number of reasons had been given for their inability to provide sufficient electrical power. One of the widely held views was that the country had not been able to set up a sound technological base to support their industrialization. This unfortunate situation has required the government-energy company to rely heavily on general importation. The lack of accountability and the failure to enforce town-planning codes were also major factors for their dismal performance. In addition, illegal connections and theft greatly worsened the situation. On the national electric's part, they blamed their inefficiency on the shortage of funds, obsolete equipment, huge debts, illegal connections, theft, increasing demands for electricity, and overloading. Unfortunately, the majority of Nigerians had to live constantly with little or no electricity when the country had built four power stations. Not being able to supply their customers, the government-owned utility company resorted to load scheduling by sharing what little power they had, ranging from two to three hours a day or in some cases none at all. In an attempt to offset these problems, the government company tried borrowing money from the World Bank, which was reluctant to give them a loan until they made drastic changes in their revenue collection and management. So rather than trying to clean up the corruption and the problems associated with the government's over involvement in the private sector, the government-owned utility company felt it was easier to borrow money and seek aid directly from leading industrialized countries like the United States, Britain, and Japan. These countries tied terms and conditions to their loans, which normally meant that the purchase of equipment and services had to be made from the country providing the loan.

The ailing utility company was also partially responsible for the high cost of goods and services in the country because it forced all companies to buy and maintain costly generators. Again, the reasons for the electrical problems were numerous, ranging from administration lapses to outright fraud. I was tempted to move out of this particular area in search of another apartment, but there was no guarantee that I would not end up in a similar or worse situation. I decided it was better to stay put and, like the majority of Nigerians, suffer in silence.

While I was trying to cope with suffering in silence, the go-slow situation had become so severe that the Lagos governor had to introduce an odd-and-even license plate system. The new system sounded logical, with odd license plates driving on one day, and even on the next; and for the first month it actually worked, but owners and drivers who had to be on the road every day found a way to beat the system. Because of the lack of accountability, it was easy to bribe and get exemption stickers indicating that they were members of the press, medical doctors, armed forces, or any sticker that would keep them on the road every day. There were too many loopholes in the system, and the traffic situation became worse than it had been before they implemented the scheme.

Returning to my own situation, I decided to pay the Simpsons a visit. I met them with the club manager while they were busy preparing for evening activities. They were planning to bring some of the current singing groups from the United States and Europe to Nigeria. This was not the first time entertainers from the United States had come to Nigeria to perform. Previous artists included Kool and the Gang, Shalamar, Millie Jackson, Roy Ayers, and Dizzy Gillespie to name a few.

About two weeks after visiting the Simpsons, I received an unexpected visit from Mrs. Simpson. She informed me that they were leaving the country on very short notice and wanted to know if I could hold on to a large suitcase of personal items until they returned.

She began by saying, "I am sorry to inconvenience you with our problems, but we had a disagreement with the club owner, and we thought it would be in our best interest to try and leave the country tonight."

Even though she tried to conceal her distress, it was obvious that they were being "encouraged" to leave the country by their former employer. With this in mind, I suggested that we return to the hotel to pick up the suitcase. As we made our way from the hotel parking lot, I had an eerie feeling that unseen eyes were watching our every move. We met Mr. Simpson hurriedly packing suitcases, and he paused for a minute to tell me the same thing his wife had just said.

I asked if there was anything I could do, and with an apologetic look he said, "No, that's it, and we appreciate you and the Colonel providing us with the opportunity of coming to Nigeria."

There was a knock at the door; it was Mike, their club manager, who wanted to have a private word with me. The suitcase was heavy, and Mike offered his assistance in helping me to take it to the car. While we were downstairs, Mike said he was packed, but he was not traveling with the Simpsons and wanted to know if he could stay with me temporarily. I felt sorry for Mike because he was a victim of circumstance, so I told him that he was more than welcome to stay. The Simpsons met us in the parking lot moments later, and once again they expressed their sorrow over what had happened, but they assured me that they would return in the near future. Mike and I said our farewells, and after leaving the hotel, I asked Mike if he knew what had happened. He indicated that the club owner was not happy about the Simpsons engaging in other business activities while under his employment.

I told Mike we had an extra guest staying with us because I had taken in Jon two weeks earlier. Jon was from the same ethnic group as the Colonel and was also in need of temporary accommodations. He was a college graduate and a middle-level manager for the Nigerian National Supply Company. This company was set up by the government in an effort to ensure that subsidized food items reached the majority of Nigerians at controlled prices. I asked Jon why Nigeria had to import food items.

He said, "In the past, Nigeria was growing enough food to feed its citizens and still had enough left over for export, but because of the oil boom, we stopped growing cash crops and started importing everything from rice to bottled water. Food prices had reached a point to where the average Nigerian could no longer afford to buy it, and the government's intention was to bring in these food items to control the prices. Unfortunately, the problems within the government only made the subsidize food prices even higher."

I was in the questioning mode, so I asked Jon why passengers traveling by trains from the west to the east had to go north before getting to their destination.

"Our railroads were designed by the British colonial government, mainly for their selfish interest of taking out the raw materials, and our government has not corrected the problem."

While we were on the subject of Nigeria, I commented on Nigeria's general problems, and Jon responded by saying, "The majority of our present problems are unnecessary, and some of us blame the British while others blame our past and present leaders. I blame the British and our leaders because they are both at fault. The British brought us together for their own benefit, and our leaders refuse to have a referendum on how we want to coexist or not coexist. So our social, economical, and political problems continue to exist at our own detriment."

Continuing with our conversation, I asked Jon why the three different ethnic groups could not get along.

"Considering how we were brought together by the British, it's amazing that we are still together. Like with other African countries, our problems began with the Berlin Conference in 1884. The conference was designed to let countries like France, Germany, Portugal, and Great Britain carve up Africa into different countries without any regard for their social and cultural boundaries. So the cause of our ethnic problems rests with the Berlin Conference, forced union by the British, and the inability of our leaders to deal with the situation."

I was curious to know how Nigeria got its name, and Jon said, "It's another reminder that our fragile union is in serious trouble. Nigeria got its name from Flora Shaw the girl friend of Lord Lugard, who was the first colonial governor of Nigeria. The name is as artificial as our forced union. They say she got the name from the River Niger, but word *Niger* has no traditional meaning with any of the ethnic groups in the country other than it was named after the Niger River."

After learning how Nigeria got its artificial name, and how they were brought together, it was easy to see why the country was struggling at nation building. I enjoyed our enlightening conversations that gave me another prospective of the Nigerian society. Jon and Mike stayed with me for about two months before finding their own lodging. I would continue to see Jon, but Mike returned to the United States shortly after moving out of the flat.

The Colonel was returning to his hometown in preparation for his new career in business and was expecting me to join him. I was not too keen on leaving

Lagos, which served not only as the country's capital, but it was also the heart of government business in Nigeria. I changed my mind a month later, but it would be too late to save the furniture or the car. Regardless of where I was going to stay, I was not going to renew the lease on the flat because of the obvious problems. It was about this time that I started having doubts about ever completing the sports-equipment contract because the new sports director was unhappy that he was not part of the initial negotiations. The negotiations dragged on until I was able to persuade him to continue with the order two months later. Once again, I had to return to the Nigerian embassy in Washington DC for payment. I told Willie that I would be near his hometown for a couple of days, and he said I was welcome to stay at his home. I accepted Willie's invitation, and after obtaining the required documents from the ministry of defense two weeks before Christmas, I left for Washington DC.

When I arrived, I went straight to the Nigerian embassy with the hope of solving all my problems in one day. I was able to see the military finance officer, and I showed him my authorization to pick up the check. He said that before payment could be made, I had to see the military attaché. I wondered why the military attaché wanted to see me because I was instructed by the Lagos office to contact the finance officer. At any rate, I was escorted to the military attaché's office, and after introductions, he challenged my identity and wanted a legal document authorizing me to represent the company. Instead of spending only a few days in Washington DC, I would now have to stay at least a week. I told the military attaché that I would have the necessary documents within five days. The brief meeting came to an end, and after thanking him, I started making my way back to the finance officer. I repeated what his boss had said, and like me, he thought it was a minor problem that could be cleared up within a week. I was able to call Willie's son Michael from his office, and within an hour we were headed toward their home in nearby Maryland. My visit to the East Coast was once again in the dead of winter, and I knew our activities would be limited.

At that time, Michael was a bachelor in his mid to late twenties, a captain in the army reserve, and an aspiring businessman assisting his father in the same manner as Mr. Grant was assisting me. I made some phone calls. The first one was to Bob's wife, Carmen. After explaining the situation, she promised to send off the power of attorney the next day. I called my family, who understood the situation, and they were looking forward to seeing me after the holidays.

I received the power of attorney within three days, but because of the other delays and the upcoming holidays, I was not able to leave until January. After quietly ringing in the New Year, I noticed a story on the international page of the *Washington Post* that gave me a mild shock. The story indicated that President Shagari's civilian government had been toppled by a military coup led by General Buhari. I showed the article to Michael, and we both looked at each other in disbelief. First, the delay with the power of attorney request, and now a military coup. There was no way we could check on Willie because the military government had cut all lines of communications, and all we could do was wait until after the holidays.

The Nigerian embassy reopened for business on the third of January. The staff seemed to be in good spirits after hearing that the military had taken power from the country's most corrupt civilian government. I spoke with the finance officer before seeing the military attaché because I was concerned that the new military government would not honor my contract. He assured me that there would be no problems and that he would call his office to see if he could get an appointment for me. Twenty minutes later, we received confirmation, and I was once again in the attaché's office. We greeted each other, and I immediately handed him the power of attorney. He was satisfied, and the next day, I received a check for another partial payment and took off for the West Coast. The delays on the East Coast had shortened the time I could spend on the West Coast; but I was able to visit with family, friends, Mr. Grant, and Bob Chang's wife. This was the shortest amount of time I had spent on the West Coast so far, but everyone was glad to see that I was not affected by the recent coup in Nigeria. I took off for Nigeria, hoping that the recent change of government would not affect my business.

Two days after returning to Lagos, the Colonel made arrangements to have the furniture, including the Simpson's large suitcase, transferred to his hometown. Since I was not going to renew my lease, I needed a temporary place to stay. I explained my situation to Willie, and he offered me a room in his duplex. Willie had recently lost his wife to an illness while she was in America, and he was struggling with this loss. A week after moving in with Willie, I received information from the Colonel's hometown that car snatchers had taken my car at gunpoint. This was another setback, but after my ill-fated sporting-goods partnership and my business with Olu, I had become immune to setbacks.

My friendship with Ada was coming to an end about the same time that I moved out of the flat. We had no emotional commitments, which made it easy for us to drift apart; however, her invaluable support in finding the flat and taking me around Lagos in her vintage Peugeot will always bring good memories. Ada and I were many things to each other, but more importantly, we were good friends.

While staying with Willie, I would occasionally ride with him to Lagos, and on the way back, he would usually stop by and see his friend Dora. Dora lived in the local government area of Surulere and was from one of the small ethnic groups in the midwestern part of the country. Dora was a successful business contractor and was receiving her share of government contracts. I had the opportunity of working on a couple of local contracts with her and Willie, and I was impressed with her business skills. Willie was fortunate to have Dora as a friend and a business associate.

Regarding the former civilian government, it was in 1982 that Nigerians realized that the Shagari government was economically crumbling; bills remained unpaid, food prices skyrocketed, and the naira lost value on a daily basis. Politics was a violent game during this period, and political opponents thought nothing of killing a political adversary through assassins, who would often use the guise of armed robbery to murder their victims.

Prior to the civil war in 1967, social crimes such as armed robbery had been almost nonexistent in Nigeria. People had a sense of concern and respect for each other's lives and property. Unlike the United States, where the majority of robberies take place while the occupants are not home, in Nigeria robbers would come in the middle of the night, ten or more at a time, giving the occupants no chance to escape. To make matters worse, the people had no confidence in the police. In some cases, the armed robbers were known to work directly or indirectly with crooked elements in the police and armed forces. Private security guards or vigilante groups were no match in confronting the men of the underworld.

Buhari's military regime arrived on the political scene intent on correcting the ills of the country with a heavy hand, but it would lead to his early retirement. In terms of the press, General Buhari wasted no time in making it known that he was in power; he jailed two *Guardian* newspaper reporters and placed them before a military tribunal in March of 1984. They had supposedly leaked information on new appointees for ambassadorships, the majority of which were military personnel. The two journalists would each eventually serve one year in prison while other members of the press were detained without trial.

Military tribunals were temporarily set up to try a number of leading politicians in an effort to show the public that they were trying to tackle corruption and the lack of accountability in the society. Some were given two to three life sentences while former president Shagari, his vice president, and a few others were kept in detention and never brought to trial.

Other decrees were tampering with oil pipelines, illegally dealing in petroleum products, armed robbery, counterfeit currencies, treason, kidnapping, lynching, drug trafficking, and possession of arms and ammunition. All of these offenses carried the death penalty.

Lynching in Nigeria was popularly known as "jungle justice." This vigilante approach to crime was also called instant justice because the person accused of the crime would receive a citizen's arrest, trial, verdict, sentence, and execution in almost the same amount of time it took to commit the crime.

One of Buahri's objective was to instill in the people a sense of unity and nationalism, but this idea was viewed as a joke because the major ethnic groups that had been forced together were still divided, and it appeared they had no desire to support what they felt was an unjust union.

Another objective was to eliminate, or at least curb, the level of corruption within the Nigerian society. I found this interesting because some of the leaders were asking Nigerians to remove corruption from the society while they made no effort to deal with their own. Toward the end of my two months' stay with

Willie, I got a surprise visit from the Colonel. After asking about my general welfare and the status of the sports-equipment order, I told him the situation was not promising because the new sports director was being difficult, and I was seriously thinking about packing up and leaving the country. The Colonel was in Lagos on personal business, which indicated that he had lost interest in doing any further business with me. He said that he would talk to the sports director and other key officers while he was in town. I knew this was a wasted effort because there was no love lost between the Colonel and the sports director; but more importantly, as I escorted him to the car, I knew that this would probably be the last time I would see the Colonel.

Two days later, a Nigerian businessman came to see Willie; and when I explained that Willie was not in, the Nigerian introduced himself as Prince Fedelis and said he had an appointment to see Willie. Sensing his disappointment, I suggested that he wait a few minutes. While we were making conversation, he indicated that he had lived in the United States for about four years, and in turn I told him that I had been coming to Nigeria since 1978. Toward the end of our conversation, we discussed the subject of accommodations. He said he couldn't wait any longer because he was in the process of moving. This caused me to mention my ongoing search for a flat, and he said I was welcome to come by and have a look at his old flat. We set an appointment for ten the following morning, and he left.

That afternoon, I informed Willie about his visitor and mentioned that I might find a vacant flat through him. Willie had no objections and said that if things did not work out, I was still welcome to stay with him until I could find a place. The next morning, I took a taxi to the local government area of Igbobi. Upon reaching the address, I could see Prince standing on the balcony, gesturing for me to come around the back and up to the flat. On the far side of the compound was an office building, and next to that was an Apostle church. I made my way to the back where I found a flight of stairs leading up to the flat. Prince offered to give me a quick tour. The first room was a small kitchen with a table, chair, and kerosene stove. He said the stove was still working if I wanted to use it. I was only bringing a few furniture items with me—which included a small bed, a portable television, and a small stereo set—so I told him I could really use the stove.

Prince said the flat had running water and a small hot water heater for the shower. I thought this was a plus. I followed Prince down the hallway, where he showed me the room he would be using until his new office was ready. The hallway opened up into a living room that contained only a small table supporting a fan and more importantly, a phone. This was an added bonus. Prince pointed to a bedroom with the same view as the living room. Of the three other bedrooms, I decided that this would be the one for me. Being satisfied with the flat, I asked Prince if the area ever had problems with armed robbers. He said no; there was an army base nearby, and the police patrolled the area during the night. With so much security, I was able to put my fears aside; but I would later learn that this was a false sense of security.

Prince told me about the other buildings in the compound.

He said, "You saw the church when you came in, and there is an office building on the other side, which makes it quite lively during the day, but it's usually quiet at night. There are tenants who live on the ground floor, but they are hardly ever in town."

The rental price was more than reasonable, and Prince said I could pay for the flat on a monthly basis. We also made an oral agreement to share the expenses of the phone and electricity bills. Prince gave me a spare key, and within thirty minutes, we had settled our business with a handshake. That evening I informed Willie that I had accepted the flat and thanked him for providing me with accommodations for the past two months. My new location was not far from the main road, and Willie said that he would drop in to see how I was doing. That next morning, I hired a minivan; and with my few belongings, I headed for number 10 Isaac John Street.

Upon reaching my new accommodations, I instructed the driver to pull into the compound. I could see Prince's Mercedes, and after greeting him upstairs, I began taking my items from the van. While I was doing so, a man walked up and asked who we were. I told him that I was working with Prince and that I would be temporarily staying in the flat. This was enough to ease his concerns, and in turn he introduced himself as Emanuel and offered to help carry the items. I was hoping to move in without attracting too much attention, but I accepted his offer with the hope that it would speed up the process. Within a short while, all of the items were upstairs. Emanuel said he would give me a call later that afternoon.

My first task was to clean up the rooms that I would be using, which included the bedroom, bathroom, and kitchen. It only took a few minutes to put the small bed together. And as I placed the short-wave portable radio on the bed, I thought of the importance of being in touch with the international world through the British Broadcasting Corporation (BBC) and the Voice of America (VOA). The short-wave radio stations provided not only the world news, but also the international business news, which included the exchange rate for the world's major currencies against the naira. The other personal item I treasured was my portable beard trimmer, which also served as hair clippers throughout my stay in Nigeria.

When I had finished cleaning, my mind drifted back to the failed business venture with Olu. The Colonel's attempt to assist us after that fiasco by providing us with the opportunity to get our first government contracts. Unfortunately, his efforts were cut short by his retirement and our inability to get a bank to honor our letters of credit.

I returned to reality upon hearing the playful sounds of children returning from school. The children looked nice in their school uniforms; with the girls wearing pullover dresses or skirts and blouses while the boys wore shorts or pants and short sleeve shirts. While I was admiring these young minds returning to their respective homes, three of the children came through the gate and headed for the back of the compound.

An hour later, Emanuel returned to see how I was doing, and I told him that I had worked up an appetite for some traditional food. Emanuel was surprised that I could eat their traditional foods. He went to the balcony and spoke to one of his two younger children playing in the compound. "John, go tell David I want to see him now—now."

Within minutes, David was upstairs. After introductions, I told him I wanted to buy some rice, beans, beef, sauce, and a 7-Up.

He replied by saying, "Rice and beans are sold by the cup, and they charge for each piece of meat, but there is no charge for the sauce."

I needed plastic food containers, and Emanuel said David could buy them from one of the nearby market women. I gave David five naira, and before long, he returned with the food containers and enough money to buy the food and a couple of sodas.

While we were waiting for David to return with the food, Emanuel gave me a little more background information on himself and his family. Emanuel was about forty-five years old, unemployed, and married to the landlady's daughter. They had four children, including a newborn. His wife and mother-in-law operated a clothing shop in the popular Balogun market. I would occasionally shop for imported clothing items, Italian sandals, cigarettes, and other items of interest at this market. Like the other major markets in Lagos, their market offered just about anything Nigerians and foreign consumers needed or wanted, from food items to clothing.

I never understood why Emanuel was released from the United African Company, the largest multinational company in Nigeria, but I got the impression that it was something that he'd rather not talk about. I told him that the majority of my business was with the army and that I was trying to complete a contract with them. It didn't take long for Emanuel to see that I was a struggling African American businessman.

David returned with the food, and after washing up, I realized there was no spoon, but luckily I found one in the kitchen. All the food was in one container, with the beans on top, and instead of mixing them with the rice, I decided to taste them first. I paused for a moment when I heard a soft crunch, and wondered why this particular bean was softer than the others.

Emanuel asked what was wrong, and after I explained he said, "Sorry, we have serious problems with boll weevil insects as a result of improper storage, the lack of insecticides, and the sorting and cleaning of the beans. I'm glad you didn't bite down on a small stone."

With the exception of the boll weevil, the food was very good, and thereafter I became a regular consumer of the traditional Nigerian foods on Isaac John Street. Prior to this, I had bought the majority of my snacks and meals from one of the major department stores because they offered Western-style meals and snacks.

Emanuel became a frequent visitor to the flat, and not a day would pass without us talking about the unnecessary ills of the country. Being an optimist, I was always offering constructive criticism to any given situation, but my positive suggestions kept falling on deaf ears. Emanuel and the majority of other Nigerians had virtually given up hope that anything positive could happen in Nigeria under its present political structure.

As my first day on Isaac John Street was coming to an end, I noticed an increase in foot traffic. Among the people returning home from work and other activities were Emanuel's wife, his eldest daughter, and a nursing baby tied to his wife's back. Emanuel insisted that I meet his wife, Kemi, who displayed a cheerful personality as she introduced me to their young daughter, and baby. After welcoming me to their compound, his wife entered one of the two bungalows in the back. I returned to the flat and told Emanuel that I would see him tomorrow.

Thirty minutes later, I decided to close the balcony door to keep the mosquitoes out. I saw an elderly woman coming through the gate. I assumed it was Emanuel's mother-in-law, and an hour later, I heard a knock on the door. When I opened it, she confirmed my suspicions as she stood on the porch with another person I had not seen before.

"Good evening. My mother is the landlady of this compound, and she wants me to ask you some questions. Can we come in?"

"Please."

"Are you paying Prince to stay here?"

"No."

"Are you sure?"

"Yes."

"Who are you?"

"I am one of his business associates from the United States."

"My mother does not like what's happening, and she wants you to tell Prince that she wants to speak with him; and she says that's it for now, but she might come back."

"I'll pass the message on."

With the exception of a couple of mosquitoes finding their mark, I was able to get through the major part of the night without any more interruptions.

Emanuel's wife and mother in-law opening the front gate on their way to the market awakened me before daybreak. The Muslims' call to prayer followed, and two hours later, I was watching Emanuel send his kids off to school.

With last night's incident still on my mind, I phoned Prince and explained my encounter with the landlady. He said he would have a talk with her. Prince must have worked his magic, or the landlady had sympathy for me because that was the only time I would hear anything from the her regarding me staying in the flat. Like the majority of Nigerians and foreigners, Prince was also working on government contracts, and he was not doing too badly. I noticed some of his English was accented with African American slang from the '70s as he briefly told me about himself. Prince lived in New York City in the mid 1970s for about five years as a student before returning to Nigeria to take advantage of the oil boom and government contracts. Prince was from a minority ethnic group in the midwestern region, and he was the first traditional prince I had the opportunity of meeting. I would eventually work with Prince on a couple of deals, but nothing ever materialized from our efforts.

By the weekend, I had settled into the new community and was ready to begin a new week. In an effort to save money, I was now sharing taxis with other passengers and riding in minivans. On rare occasions, I would put my heart in my hand and climb aboard the notorious molue bus. This vehicle and the minivans would only stop at major bus stops, which required walking farther distances to my destinations, but I didn't mind because it provided another opportunity to mingle with the people and exercise at the same time.

After spending the day at the ministry of defense and visiting other government offices in the area, I took a taxi to Isaac John Street. While I was walking toward the flat, I noticed that the foot traffic was slowing down for someone getting out of a taxi not far from the compound. As I came closer, I could see it was a tomboyish young girl, hurriedly trying to gather her belongings while a few other pedestrians and I waited impatiently to let her finish for safety reasons. These precautions were necessary because the majority of the residential streets in Lagos had no sidewalks, forcing pedestrians to use the streets. The girl carried a sports bag and appeared to be an athlete. When she finished collecting her items, she excused herself, and I told her it was okay because I lived nearby.

She said, "Hi, I'm Kuby. Are you an American?"

I said yes and moved away from the other pedestrians who were less patient.

I asked her what sport she played, and she held up a table tennis paddle and said, "Table tennis. I play for Nigeria's national team."

During our brief conversation, I noticed an older male occupant slowly getting out from the other side of the taxi. It was only after paying off the taxi that he noticed his daughter talking to me.

From his facial expressions, I could tell he was not going to let us finish the conversation, so I tried to end it by saying, "Nice meeting you."

With a big smile she said, "That's my father. He's like that with everyone I meet."

Using American slang she said, "I'll see you later."

I smiled and walked away hoping that I didn't offend her father, but I could tell from the look in his eyes that I would be suspect as long as I lived on Isaac John Street.

I would eventually find out that Kuby's father was obsessively following her table tennis career to a fault. Two days after I met Kuby, her father surprisingly came to the compound in the morning, yelling in Yoruba, and pointing toward the flat. Until now, I was enjoying another serene African morning as I prepared for another day in Lagos.

Even though I knew very little of the Yoruba language, it sounded like he was saying, "I know Kuby is up there with that American, and I want you to come down now."

Knowing that he was talking about me, I went downstairs. Emanuel, who was also alerted by the yelling, spoke to Kuby's father in Yoruba.

With a slight grin, Emanuel said, "Now, the old man thinks that Kuby is upstairs."

Being a suspect from our first meeting was not helping me at this time, Emanuel translated to him that his daughter was not there, and I invited him inside the flat. He refused to enter and left looking dejected because he could not confirm his suspicion.

Later that day, Kuby, unaware that her father had been to the compound, came by the flat after attending school and table tennis practice. I told her what had happened with her father that morning, and that it made me feel uncomfortable because he was getting the wrong impression of me. She apologized for the incident and said it wouldn't happen again. Feeling even more uncomfortable with her being in the flat, I suggested that in order for us to continue this cultural exchange, it would be better if we could communicate over the phone instead of visiting. She agreed, and during my six-month stay on Isaac John Street, Kuby would call often to talk about everything from the latest rap craze to what it was like growing up as a teenager in America. When there was no phone and she wanted to know more about African Americans and the United States, she would defy her father's wishes and find her way to the flat.

It was through phone conversations, chance meetings, and sometimes through visits that were against my wishes that she told me what it was like growing up as a teenager in Nigeria. She began by telling me that her mother died shortly after her birth, and her father brought her up in the Muslim faith. When I arrived on Isaac John Street, Kuby was Nigeria's Junior champion, and her young table tennis career had provided her the opportunity to visit China, Egypt, England, Germany, and the former Soviet Union. Like most Nigerians, Kuby was fed up with military rule and all the other problems facing the country. Her desire was to use her table tennis career and leave Nigeria as soon as possible.

In exchange, I told her what it would be like if she grew up as an teenager in the United States, and she was impressed but indicated that she wanted to visit Britain first because they had professional table tennis. It was through Kuby that I met Toby, her older brother, and we established a long friendship. Unfortunately, I would lose contact with Kuby after I left Isaac John Street, but I stayed in touch with Toby. Shortly before I left Nigeria in 1995, he told me that Kuby was playing professional table tennis in Britain and doing quite well.

As I continued to pursue my business interests with the ministry of defense, I would occasionally run into Uloma. During our brief meetings, we would inquire about each other's welfare and update each other on our present addresses. In our brief meetings, we made promises to visit each other, but because we were both chasing unpaid contracts and other interests in our lives, we never made good on our promises.

Before I knew it, four months had passed. Emanuel came to me one Friday afternoon and said, "I'm working on a hot deal; will you be interested?"

"What kind of hot deal?"

"One that will make us some clean money. But I will be able to tell you more in a couple of weeks."

Although this hot deal had all the markings of a scam, I was curious to see how he was going to produce "clean money."

It was the beginning of another weekend, and having no social invitations, I decided to spend the evening watching television. I fell asleep during a late-night movie and was awakened around 2:00 AM by what I thought was a family argument. The television station was making a static sound because it had gone off the air. I turned off the television, and after covering myself again with a sheet to ward off the mosquitoes, I tried going back to sleep. It wasn't long before my sleep was once again interrupted. This time it was the sound of breaking bottles.

I stepped out onto the balcony to see what was happening and heard someone telling a security guard, "Stay still, or I take your life."

This could only mean armed robbers were in the area, so I quickly went back inside.

While I was trying to get a better view from the living-room window, I heard more breaking bottles. Their target was a woman screaming in terror as she tried to escape onto her balcony. Unfortunately, the armed robbers had an ample supply of bottle ammunition from the vendor's empties to be picked up the following day. The escape route was cut off, which left the barefoot woman with no alternative but to painfully retreat over broken glass back to the other armed robbers she was trying to flee from.

Fifteen minutes later, I saw the leader and his henchmen leaving the compound after relieving many of the occupants of their money and other valuables. It appeared they were headed in my direction. I thought of calling the police, but time was not on my side. I had to make a decision to stay or run.

I heard the leader say in pidgin English, "Na dis be de the boy-oh-boy gang," (This is the boy-oh-boy gang) as he fired off a round into the air for good measure.

Moving quickly, I started making my way downstairs to inform the other residents of the situation. I went to Emanuel's door first, but after several knocks and no response, I tried the door of the landlady's son. Again, there was no response. I was about to return to the flat, but the door opened, and standing there rubbing the sleep from his eyes was the landlady's son. "What's happening?" I told him that armed robbers were in the area, and he threw on a rap cloth and made his way to the front of the compound without wearing slippers. I followed from a safe distance with slippers. I guessed the excitement of wanting to see the armed robbers in action had overtaken landlady's son's rational thinking; he was now standing in the spotlight of the compound's security lights, which made him an easy target for the robbers.

It wasn't long before an empty bottle flew over the security wall and broke near his feet. He was too petrified to move until the second bottle whistled passed his head that came with an accompanying voice, "Go back, we did not come for you." He quickly became unfrozen, and in his haste to leave, he forgot about the broken glass on the pavement. I cringed every time he stepped on a jagged piece of glass as he painfully retreated to his room.

While the landlady's son was nursing his wounds, I continued looking for a place to hide from the armed robbers. I found what I thought was a secure area between Emanuel's bungalow and a security wall. It was a tight fit, but I was determined to wait until the armed robbers had left the area.

Twenty minutes later, and not knowing where I was hiding, I heard Emanuel saying, "The armed robbers had left the area, and it's safe to come out."

This was good news, and when Emanuel noticed that I was climbing out from in between the two cement walls, he started laughing and said, "Trying to hide outside of the flat only increases the chances of being seen by the armed robbers or being accused by the residents as being one of them. So it's better to stay inside." I thought to myself that this is a no win situation.

It would not be until 8:00 AM that following morning that we would see the police, which gave a new meaning to slow-response times.

As Emanuel and I were talking about our early-morning visit from the armed robbers, a hungry petty thief who was unaware that armed robbers were recently in the area tried to steal a loaf of bread from one of the local vendors. Unfortunately, the thief was ripe for jungle justice, and he was chased and beaten with sticks, stones, and anything else the crowd could get their hands on. He would have been killed if a Good Samaritan had not intervened to save the man's life. Within twenty-four hours, I had seen an armed robbery and a man nearly beaten to death for stealing a loaf of bread.

Two weeks had passed, and it was time for Emanuel to tell me about the deal of a lifetime.

"You remember that hot deal I told you about two weeks ago?"

"Yes, I've been waiting."

"I have a friend who works in the Nigerian minting company, and he has access to negative five-naira notes."

At that time, the paper currency in Nigeria consisted of one-, five-, ten-, and twenty-naira notes.

"What do you mean 'negative notes'?" I asked.

"It means that the notes have not been fully developed. The good part about this deal is that the notes are free, but we have to pay for the liquid chemicals required to wash the color off the negatives. Once that's done, we will have original five-naira notes."

"How much do the chemicals cost?"

"The least amount we can buy is twelve thousand naira, but our profit would be around fifty-five thousand or sixty thousand naira."

"You said 'our' profit. How many people are involved?"

"Three, and our initial investment will be shared equally, so all you have to come up with is four thousand naira."

He said his friend was waiting downstairs to give us a demonstration in his living room. As we entered Emanuel's living room, I could see the props were laid out, and his "partner-in-crime" was dressed in a beige safari suit and standing proudly behind a small table. On the table was a display of five five-naira negatives notes, a small glass bottle containing a clear liquid, a towel, and a pan of water. After introductions, Emanuel's friend started explaining the tools of their scam by holding up the negative of a five-naira note with a regular five note to show that they were of the same size. Adding to the special effects, he put on a pair of latex gloves and removed the cap to what he described as the chemicals required to wash the negatives. He ran the open container under my nose, and I detected a scent of alcohol. After washing the negative notes with the chemicals and rinsing them in the pan of water, the negative notes appeared to be the official currency.

The only thing missing in this scam was my share of the twelve thousand naira. Having seen how this scam was going produce clean money, I thanked Emanuel for the demonstration and told him that I was not interested in the deal.

As I was making my way out of his living room, Emanuel said, "It's a good deal! We can't lose, and I think you should give it some more time. I'll get back to you later."

Again, I told them I was not interested, and after returning to the flat, I knew my days on Isaac John Street were coming to an end; and I saw very little of Emanuel before leaving Isaac John Street.

After returning from Lagos city one weekday afternoon, I overheard a female voice asking one of the children if I lived in the compound. Naturally, this drew my attention, so I went to the balcony, and to my surprise it was Carole and another person. I directed them to the back, and after a warm greeting, she introduced me to her friend Pius. I was curious as to how she was able to find me, and she said it was through a mutual friend I had met back in '82. The flat looked the same as it had when I first moved in, and while I tried to apologize, Carole suggested that I take a ride with them to their place because we had a lot to talk about.

Pius was driving a late model 504 Peugeot. And for a moment, it reminded me of the misfortune I had with my Peugeot. We were now in the local government of Ogba, and it wasn't long before Pius pulled through an open gate to the compound. After parking, he decided to give us some time together, and asked Carole to let him know when I was ready to go. Carole told me that she lived upstairs, and upon reaching her door, I noticed that it was open.

She said, "Come on, it's my children trying to catch a breeze because there is probably no light."

Carole introduced me to her daughter Mary; who had just finished college, her son Tony, who was preparing to enter college; and her younger son Kenny, who was in grade school. Carole said she wanted to offer refreshments, but their area had been without electricity for two days. Having adjusted to the lack of constant electrical supply, I told her that I was used to not having power all the time.

It was obvious that Carole had taken good care of herself. I was surprised to see that she had three children of whom two were young adults. We moved to the dining area, and the first question she asked was about James and his brother. I explained to Carole that I hadn't spoken to James since '79, and I went on to tell her of the events leading to Isaac John Street. In regards to her own well-being, she indicated that she would occasionally get small contracts through federal, state, and local governments; but the economy was becoming worse and contracts harder to find. Carole was divorced and doing a good job of raising her children with some financial assistance from her ex-husband. I asked her about Taiwo, and she said she had married a medical doctor and was living in England. I thought it was time to be heading back, so Carole led me to Pius's flat, which was located on the ground floor in the back.

After seeing me downstairs to Pius's flat, where he was patiently waiting for us, Carole told me she would not be making the return trip with Pius and reminded me to stay in touch. Pius started off by apologizing for the lack of electricity, but I told him he did not have to apologize for something that he had no control of. My remarks put him at ease, and we continued our conversation. I told him what had brought me to the country and how I was now like the average businessman in Nigeria because I was doing a little bit of everything as long as it was legal. In return, he told me he was working with his uncle, producing plastic belts mainly for schoolchildren.

Pius gave me a tour of his operation, and I was surprised to see that he was accomplishing this task out of his bedroom. He pointed out the major items, which were on a small worktable that served as the base for a rivet machine, a hole puncher, and a pair of heavy-duty scissors. Along the sides of the wall were bundles of bulk plastic strips that came in different widths and colors, with plastic buckles to match. Pius said his function in the company was to clear the semifinished material through customs, assemble the belts, and once he had enough for shipment, transport them in his car to the eastern city of Enugu, where his uncle sold them to wholesalers in the area. I was impressed with their plastic belt operation but disappointed that he and other Nigerians had to import finished and semifinished goods after exporting their raw materials to the United States, Britain, and other industrialized countries.

The other negative aspect about this operation was that it required traveling on Nigerian highways, which was risky business because sections of the roads were not safe, and there were armed robbers and illegal police checkpoints along the way. The personal tour had come to an end, and Pius said he had an appointment not far from my flat and offered to take me back. Before dropping me off, he said that he would be coming by to see how I was doing.

A week later, Pius came by the flat and suggested I take a ride with him to his place in Ogba. Shortly after we began our journey, he said he was having problems with his uncle and was thinking about starting his own plastic belt business. I had reservations about Pius attempting to start his own operation using the same suppliers and distributors.

I asked if he was sure that was what he wanted to do, and he said, "I'm doing a lot of different jobs for my uncle. I clear the goods from customs, I make the belts, and I transport them to the east. I have given him more than enough time to give me an increase, and he keeps telling me to hold on while he continues to make more money."

By the time we reached his flat, he had already made up his mind, and the only thing I could do was support his move. Pius broke out two beers, and after reinforcing his reasons for leaving his uncle's business, he showed me his photo album. For the next two hours, he pointed out the people of importance to him. There was one particular photo of a woman that caught my attention, and I asked who she was.

"That's my cousin Ninna. She's a schoolteacher, single, and the next time I travel home, I will tell her about you."

Three weeks later, Pius came by after returning from a road trip to the east with two young ladies, and one of them was Ninna. Pius knew the condition of the flat and decided it would be better if the young ladies waited in the car. He informed me that I should start preparing for an evening out on the town.

We returned to the car, and Pius introduced me to Ninna, who was even more beautiful than I had expected after seeing her photo. After we welcomed the women to Lagos, Pius said the three of them would return to pick me up after the young ladies had rested and refreshed themselves from their journey.

As promised, they returned four hours later, and we took off for a night of entertainment in the city of Ikeja. While trying to decide which nightclub to go to, we came across a private party on Ikeja's popular Allen Avenue. We were invited in, and with the DJ playing the latest hits from the United States and Nigeria, we decided to rock the night away.

This was the first time I had seen Ninna standing. Once again, I was impressed. She was around five-foot seven, in her midtwenties, and very attractive. As we danced and conversed our way through the evening, I discovered she also had a charming personality. After leaving the club, we headed for Pius's place, where Ninna and I ended up spending one of the most enjoyable weekends of our lives. On Sunday morning, we took the young ladies to the transportation depot for their five-hour bus trip to the east. This marked the beginning of our relationship, which continued for almost two years through Ninna's monthly visits. Before Pius dropped me off, he suggested sharing his flat with me and keeping the flat on Isaac John Street as an office. Pius's living conditions were better than mine, so I told him we could talk more when I returned from the United States after my daughter's high school graduation.

I left for America on June 1, 1985; and upon arriving on the West Coast, my daughter, family members, and Mr. Grant expressed concerns for my safety because of the recent military coup. I assured them that my life was never in danger and that I was planning to return in two weeks. Eventually they were able to relax their concerns. I enjoyed the brief stay and my daughter's graduation. When I returned to Nigeria, I decided to take Pius up on his offer to share accommodations. I continued using the flat on Isaac John Street for another month before letting it go. Pius and I got along like brothers, and he was good cook as well.

Chapter Four

Another Coup

In 1985, the Buhari's military regime continued to show contempt for human rights. It terrorized its citizens with its mass detentions, inflexibility, abuse of power, and harsh prison sentences. It was therefore no surprise to hear the familiar sound of military music and the subsequent announcement of yet another coup on August 27, 1985. The new military head of state, Major Gen. Ibrahim B. Babangida, popularly known as IBB, explained to the Nigerian people in a general statement why his military regime took over the government, "It is now abundantly clear, after precisely twenty months, that the present leadership lacks the capability to lead this nation out of its social and economic predicament."

After experiencing one civilian government takeover and one military coup in less than two years, the Nigerian people greeted IBB with caution. However, he would become Nigeria's second longest-serving military head of state before being forced to resign in 1993. IBB was known as a political leader, a master tactician, and an evil genius.

Upon assuming office, IBB ordered the release of a number of political detainees and put former president Shagari and his vice president on trial for corruption during their terms in office. After a speedy two-week trial, the most corrupt civilian government in Nigerian history was found not guilty. There was some opposition to the verdict, but it quickly died down because the majority of Nigerians felt Shagari was too honest to steal but not strong enough to stop some of the members of his administration from doing so. IBB also appointed a presidential committee to supervise a public debate on the controversial International Monetary Fund (IMF) loan. One of the conditions that the IMF required before granting Nigeria a loan was the removal of subsidies on the pump price of gasoline and aviation fuel. Other conditions the IMF addressed through their Structural Adjustment Program (SAP) were the overvalued naira, government over involvement in the private sector, mass corruption, and mismanagement. When the committee finished its report, it was clear that the majority of Nigerians did not want the government to accept the IMF loan. Nigeria's financial troubles started in the mid 1970s after the oil boom, and their relations with the IMF begun in 1983 when the IMF signed an agreement to refinance about two billion dollars of past debts owed by Nigerian commercial banks.

Some Nigerians felt that the rejection of the IMF loan was a blessing in disguise because it kept the nearly three-billion-dollar loan from being misused by their leaders. With the IMF officially turned down, IBB introduced his SAP on October 1, 1985. The SAP policies were basically the same as the IMF's conditions, but the Nigerian government was applying these economic measures. Unfortunately, Nigerians felt SAP was sapping what little mental and physical resolve they had left.

While Nigeria was trying to deal with the SAP, the long-smoldering religious problems once again came to the fore. Rumors circulated that IBB's military regime had joined the Organization of Islamic Countries (OIC). IBB denied this accusation and stated that the government would not impose any religion on Nigerians. This did not sit well with the Christian Association of Nigeria (CAN), headed by Catholic Archbishop Dr. Okogie. Even after these government statements, the Christian community remained uneasy because they suspected that the Muslim-led government had actually joined the OIC and then quietly withdrawn only after strong opposition from the Christians.

All Nigerian governments were far from being successful in their attempts to appear as a secular state. They would often over- or undercompensate one of the two major religions, thereby creating a never-ending adjustment policy. For example, if the Christians got three holidays a year, the Muslims would also get three; if the local, state, or federal government built a mosque, they had to build a church as well; if they subsidized trips for Christians to visit Jerusalem, they did likewise for the Muslims to visit Saudi Arabia. The country was able to overcome this OIC crisis, but the religious tension in the country was ready to erupt at the slightness provocation.

With the military running the country the majority of the time, it was not unusual to hear of an attempted coup or that the government had been overthrown. A good example of this was when the IBB regime uncovered a plot to depose their administration. The leader of the coup, General Vatsa, and fifteen other officers were convicted and sentenced to death by firing squad in February 1986. The more fortunate military officers and soldiers were given prison sentences or dismissed from the armed forces.

With all of Nigeria's upheavals and the other social troubles of the country, it was easy to overlook the achievements of the Nigerians. The country has produced scientists, intellectuals, writers, and international entertainers. Wole Soyinka (Yoruba), who was awarded the Nobel Prize for Literature in November

1986, used his writings to speak out against corruption, military rule, the abuse of human rights, and other injustices in Nigeria. His plea for peace and his critical assessment of Nigeria's civil war resulted in his arrest and imprisonment without trial from 1967 to 1969 under the Gowon military government. During his two-year incarceration, he produced one of his greatest works, *A Shuttle in the Crypt*, which is an account of Nigeria's vital history between 1966 and 1971. Since that time, he has continued to use his literary works to improve the lives of the average Nigerian. Another great Nigerian writer of conscious was Chinua Achebe (Ibo), who was born in 1930 and, like Soyinka, was a poet and attended the University of Ibadan. His first novel, *Things Fall Apart* (1958), was written as a refutation of the inaccuracies of British authors in their characterizations of Africa and its cultures. This novel spoke from the perspective of the colonized rather than the colonizer. The more popular Nigerian athletes were the late Dick Tiger (Ibo), who was the world light-heavyweight and middleweight champion in the 1950s and 1960s. Hakeem Olajuwon (Yoruba) led the Houston Rockets basketball team to two National Basketball Association (NBA) championships in 1994 and 1995. Chris Okoye (Ibo) played for the Kansas City Chiefs in the National Football League.

One of the more popular entertainers was Mr. Fela Ransome-Kuti (Yoruba), a popular bandleader used his pidgin English lyrics to criticize military regimes and the country's corrupt civilian government. His Afro-beat music was a blend of soul, jazz, and highlife (Western big-band sound combined with traditional music). His use of pidgin English allowed him to reach a wide audience of Nigerians and other Anglophone Africans. He was also known for marrying twenty-seven women at the same time. After serving twenty months in prison on drug charges, he divorced them all because he no longer believed in the institution of marriage.

Artists, writers, and intellectuals who spoke out against the government were often in danger of retaliation. On October 19, 1986, a parcel bomb killed Dele Giwa, the editor and cofounder of the popular *Newswatch* investigative news magazine. Suspicion fell on the military government because it was rumored that the editor was on to a hot story that could have implicated some high-level people in the military regime, including IBB himself.

It's unfortunate that past and present governments have not been able to harness the human and natural resources for the benefit of Nigerians. A good number of Nigerian professionals that included doctors, engineers, lawyers, writers, and educators felt they had no choice other than to leave Nigeria in order to work in a free and safe society. This brain drain had a devastating effect on Nigerian society. To make matters worse, many of these professionals were trained at the government's expense.

However, for most citizens, life went on as usual. My new roommate Pius and I had our normal Saturday-morning routine, during which we would clean the flat and prepare ourselves for the coming week. Since we had no hired house help, this included washing and ironing our clothes. On this particular Saturday, we had just finished our chores when Dora and a friend she introduced as Lucy paid us a surprise visit. I had not seen Dora since she gave a surprise birthday party for Willie, who was noticeably absent. Dora had overcome this embarrassing moment, and now it appeared she was trying to play cupid for her attractive middle-aged friend. I offered them refreshments, but Dora told me that they just dropped by so she could introduce her friend, who lived not far from us. She said her friend was in the last stages of mourning for her late husband, and she felt it would be a good idea for us to meet. I immediately felt sorry for her and offered my sympathy and assistance if she needed it. Their visit was short, and before leaving Lucy thanked me for the support and said that she would return soon.

A week later, Dora came by to ask me for a favor. At first I thought she wanted to introduce me to another grieving widow, but this time she came on her own behalf. She wanted me to talk to Willie with the hope that he might change his mind about ending their relationship. It appeared to be a desperate situation because Dora insisted that I use her hired taxi, and she would wait until I returned. I made the short ride to Willie's place, and after explaining my mission, he said in no uncertain terms that his relationship with Dora was over. I returned with the sad news, and as she held back the tears, she thanked me for trying to help. It was the last time I would see Dora, but I would hear later, through Lucy, that she was doing quite well as businesswoman in London.

The following weekend, Lucy came by and invited me to her flat, where I had the opportunity of meeting her daughter Bumi and an extended member of the family named Mora. Lucy was the personal secretary to Mr. Ernest Shonekan, the chairman of the United African Company (UAC), the largest trading company in Nigeria. Lucy told me that she had obtained her secretarial and administrative skills in London before returning to Nigeria in the mid-1970s. She was part of a middle class that had emerged during the late '70s and early '80s, but the harsh economic period was quickly diminishing their economic gains. Even with these setbacks, she was doing quite well; she had recently purchased a home in the suburbs of Lagos and had two cars. I told her what had brought me to Nigeria and that in spite of the present problems, I still had a lot of hope for the country.

It was getting late, and while she was driving me back, she asked if I could drive them to their destinations during the week, which meant driving the girls to school and her job. I could then use the car until it was time to pick them up, and she would drop me off in the evenings at Pius's flat. Still feeling sympathy for her, I told her it sounded like a good idea and that I would give it a try. In the beginning, the arrangement worked to our mutual benefit, and in the first two weeks she introduced me to her family, which included her brother Dr.

Okogie, the Catholic archbishop of Lagos. I enjoyed my conversations with the Catholic archbishop who was an open critic of military rule and past and present governments.

One day while I was waiting to pick up Lucy from her workplace, a Nigerian man walked up to the car, and to my surprise it was Olu. We recognized each other at about the same time, and I could tell that not only had he lost some weight, but he had also lost the air of confidence he had when I first met him. I asked how he had been doing, and he said that he was also doing okay, but we both knew things were not what they could be. I wanted to tell him that things were so bad that I was looking for the two thousand dollars he had left in my room in 1978, but instead I told him that I was doing okay, and that I was waiting to pick up a friend. Our conversation was cut short as Lucy arrived, and Olu smiled as we drove away. I had forgotten about Olu until this encounter, and by the time I drove Lucy home and told her how I met Olu, it was easy to once again put him in the past.

For the next two years, I became a lot of things to Lucy, including a sympathetic part time live-in companion and her driver. Unfortunately, the strain of dealing with the go-slow, the lack of business, and our differences would inevitably bring this multifaceted relationship to an end. And the situation only became worse when, with great difficulty, I had to tell her that I was not the man she was looking for.

On May 9, 1987, while IBB struggled to keep Nigeria united, it was reported that Chief Obafemi Awolowo, a former presidential candidate, had died. His socialist views did not take hold in Nigeria's capitalistic society, but he did achieve some success when it came to free education in the western region.

While all of this was happening, I had to renew one of my three-month business visas. Instead of traveling to the United States to renew it, Pius and I drove to the border town of Cotonou in the former French colony of the People's Republic of Benin. It was easy to see why smuggling was so rampant. We headed back after picking up some personal items, and more importantly, I could once again legally operate in the country for another three months.

In 1987, IBB's wife introduced one of the most successful plans under his administration, the Better Life Program. She wanted to improve the living and working conditions of Nigerian women. The Better Life Program would achieve success in bringing awareness to the Nigerian women, but when IBB was forced to resign in 1993, the social program was left to wither and eventually die.

There was not much happening in the way of business for Pius or me. His plastic belt business had failed, mainly because he could not compete against his uncle. Pius had an added worry, which was the pressure from his parents and relatives to get married. The major reason why Pius and many other Nigerian men were delaying their marriage plans was because the country was experiencing a tough economic period, and IBB's Structural Adjustment Program was having little or no effect on the economy. As a result, the cost of marriage was more than most men could afford. The majority of the young men resigned to stay single. This situation was turning young men into middle-aged bachelors and young maidens into spinsters.

Pius was able to make a little money by using his car as a *cabu-cabu* (illegal taxi), which meant he had to try and avoid the traffic wardens, better known as "yellow fever" because of their nagging mosquito-like habit of sucking what little money these illegal taxis made. Pius managed to avoid them the majority of the time, but occasionally he would get caught; luckily, with just a quick bribe, he would be off again.

As a result of my financial situation, I let myself become a willing victim to a crime known as the "advance fee" fraud (fraudulently taking money on false pretenses). It was popularly known as 419, simply because that is the number it fell under in the Nigerian police-crime book. The majority of these perpetrators carried titles like doctor (academic), professor, prince, chief, or any other title they felt would impress their unsuspecting victims. All of their deals were based on a promise that they could deliver whatever you wanted, including a shipload of oil.

My 419 experience began when Pius said he ran into a friend who might be able to help with the balance of my contract with the army. I welcomed the idea because I had lost contact with the Colonel, and since that time, I had not been able to renew any contacts with the government. The following evening, Pius and I went to see his friend, who was known as Emmanuel. He lived in a modest bungalow, and I thought nothing about meeting him at home rather than in an office because the majority of business contracts were approved outside of the workplace. After introductions, we began with a light conversation that led into the business at hand. While we were talking, another man arrived, and Emmanuel introduced him as Prince. Emmanuel suggested that the four of us go to his bedroom for more privacy. This should have set off alarms, but I was desperate to improve my financial situation.

The conversation started off with Emmanuel saying, "Pius has told me that you're having some problems collecting your money from the army."

"Yes, it's about sixty thousand dollars, and I also wanted to know if you could help with securing other government contracts."

"I can help, but I presently have a deal for a foreign company that would make you forget about the money the army owes you."

"I'm listening."

"There were a number of foreign companies that were blacklisted by the former Buhari regime, and even though some of them completed their jobs, they had to leave the country because of fraudulent activities."

"But isn't that what we're doing?"

"No, because some of these funds were already taken from the Central Bank and placed into a government foreign bank in preparation of paying off the foreign companies, but since they were blacklisted, they can't collect. We have contacts in the Central Bank who can authorize the release of the funds."

"How much money are we talking about?"

"This deal is worth forty-eight million dollars, and after the transfer has been made to your bank account, we will split profits with your company. If you are interested, we will need several blank letterheads with your signature on them, and we will fill in the rest along with the necessary government approvals. By the way, to help expedite this deal, Prince will need to travel with you to the United States. Is it possible for your company to pay for his fare?"

"I'll have to contact my associate in America, but I will give you an answer in a few days."

The next day, I informed Mr. Grant that I was working on a hot deal, and he made arrangements to wire a round-trip ticket for Prince. For the next three weeks, we held a number of meetings, and each one provided just enough information to keep me going until the next meeting. By the third week, I told them that I had received the round trip-ticket for Prince, and two days later, I received copies of the approved documents, including the typed information on my own letterhead. The following week, in early September of 1987, Prince and I took off for Oakland, California. We arrived on a Sunday afternoon, and on hand to meet us at the airport were Mr. Grant and MacArthur Lane. I thought nothing of seeing MacArthur with Mr. Grant because we had known each other from grade school, and I had followed his professional football career. We finished registering Prince in the hotel, and before we left, he once again explained how the transfer was going to work.

"My associates have already started working on the transfer, and we are just waiting for approval from the Nigerian Central Bank to release the funds from a bank in New York. I will be able to check the progress tomorrow morning, but I want you guys to know that I am at your mercy because my people are relying on me to protect their interest."

He was assured that he had nothing to fear, and as we were walking out, he wanted to know where he could get a couple of spare parts for his Mercedes Benz. MacArthur agreed to help him find the parts for his Mercedes the next day. Mr. Grant took care of the expense for his hotel accommodations.

The next morning we met in Prince's room once again. He said he had received a call from Lagos during the night, and his people said the money was being transferred, so we could check with our bank tomorrow. We decided to return the following morning for business, but socially, we continued to give Prince the royal treatment. MacArthur took Prince to find spare parts for his Mercedes Benz, and later that evening I arranged for a social outing with some friends for Prince. The next morning, the three of us waited anxiously in the bank as Mr. Grant inquired about the forty-eight-million-dollar transfer. Ten minutes later, Mr. Grant returned and said no transfer had been made, and perhaps it would be better if we checked back later that afternoon or tomorrow morning. Again, we thought it was better to come back the following morning. The next morning, Prince told us why the transfer had not been made.

"Our people at the Central Bank have informed me that the reason they have not made the transfer is because the government will not release the money until we pay a 1 percent transfer tax."

The losses up to this point had only been a round trip ticket, some Mercedes Benz spare parts, and his accommodations. We now knew the deal was bogus, and that's when the royal treatment for Prince came to a halt. For the next two days, Prince tried to convince me to tell Mr. Grant and MacArthur to come up with the 1 percent tax. I told him that MacArthur wanted to give him more than a 1 percent transfer tax and that it was in his best interest to leave the country as soon as possible. Two days later Prince was gone.

This was yet another sign for me to give up on Nigeria, but I would do just the opposite. I told Mr. Grant that I was going to make one more trip to Nigeria, and he said he would continue to assist in whatever way he could. I had some extra time on this trip, so I spent a weekend with my sister and her husband. One of their neighbors came by and was introduced as Jesse Williams.

In our conversation, I told him about my recent trip to Nigeria, and to my surprise he said, "I am glad I met you because my friend and I will be doing a cycling tour of West Africa this summer."

At that time, Jesse was a physical education teacher, and his friend, Dr. Ed Valeau, was dean of the Language Arts Learning Resources Division at Skyline College in Oakland.

The Cultural Exchange Bicycle Tour was going to take them to the major cities, like Abidjan, Accra, Lome, Cotonou, Lagos, and a host of villages along the way. I asked how they were going to carry all of their equipment.

Jesse laughed and said, "We'll be towing bike trailers with us, and they will hold our food packets, sleeping cots, mosquito nets, and the cultural exchange material."

I liked their idea, and the thought of making this journey on bikes made it even more interesting. But even though they had taken the necessary precautions against contracting malaria, I still had concerns for the malaria-carrying mosquitoes. However, it appeared Jesse and his friend were all set to pedal their way through West Africa. Some of their goals were the following:

1. Promote a dialogue between West Africa and America related to language, culture, and education.
2. Learn about the customs, history, art, and cultures of West African states in order to improve communication and understanding.
3. Broaden their understanding of the educational and cultural systems in various West African countries.

We would have several more discussions before I left for Lagos, and I indicated that I would pass their cycling event information on to the appropriate ministries in Nigeria. Three weeks later, I was back in Lagos. When I returned to Nigeria, I related my 419 experience to Pius, and he seemed a little surprised that Prince and Emmanuel were trying to collect money from Mr. Grant. Pius was obviously desperate to overcome his economic hardships because he knew that Mr. Grant was not only my business associate but also a mentor, coach, and friend. Since I was sharing the flat with Pius, I decided to put the incident behind me, but I had to start preparing myself for another move.

A week later, while Pius and I were trying to play down the 419 incident, a comical situation occurred, and it helped us to ease our tensions. The midmorning silence was shattered by the sound of breaking glass coming from the apartment above ours. At first we thought it was a stray rock from one of the kids playing in the area until we heard the sound of another rock finding its target.

The thought of armed robbers crossed our minds as we moved quietly toward the window to get a better view. That was when we saw a crying woman throwing rocks at the upstairs flat, and even though she was speaking in Yoruba, it was easy to tell she had caught her husband with another woman. It seemed the cheating husband was so preoccupied in his love nest that he didn't know what was happening until it was too late. His wife, with admirable forethought, had quietly let all the air out of his Mercedes's tires, and after strategically putting rocks into piles around the apartment, she shattered her way into her husband's illicit romance by breaking every window in the flat.

By this time, she had attracted not only our attention, but also the attention of the neighbors and anyone else in the area. The guilty and embarrassed husband thought his chances would be better if he made a run for it, so he dashed out of the apartment and headed for his car. Upon reaching it, however, he quickly realized that it would be difficult trying to get away on four flat tires. He felt his only chance now was to try to run past his rock-throwing wife.

Realizing that she could not chase him down, she started shouting, "Ole! Ole! Ole!" (Thief! thief! thief!) Within seconds, the residents who heard this cry cut off his escape route! As the crowd prepared to carry out their jungle justice, the emotionally wounded woman was able to convince the crowd that he was just a cheating husband and not a thief. Thanks to Carole, Pius, and several other neighbors, the man was saved from jungle justice.

Returning to our present situation, Pius's illegal taxi business was not generating the income he had anticipated due to the "yellow fever" sucking away at his profits, and to make matters worse, his car was spending more time in the mechanic's shop than on the road. My situation was no better because the small local contracts I came across were just barely enough to keep me going until I could get my hands on another one. If there was ever a time I wanted to leave Nigeria, it was during this time. Hard times were affecting us all, and Carole decided to take her youngest son back to her hometown in the midwest while her daughter and son stayed to complete their one-year youth service and college respectively. This was the last time I would see Carole, and it marked the end of an era that I associated with my introduction into Nigeria.

Chapter Five

On the Move

In spite of Nigeria's difficulties, I made the decision to stay on in the country, ever hopeful that another major contract was just around the corner. My occasional meetings with Uloma had grown further and further apart, until Willie dropped by one day to tell me that he had run into her at the ministry of defense. This was the second time Willie had seen Uloma, but this time instead of just telling him to pass on her greetings, she gave him her address and phone number. Willie was going into Lagos the next morning and said that if I didn't mind riding along for a couple of stops, we could stop by and see Uloma on our way back. I could have gone by myself, but Willie and I had not seen each other for a while, and I thought it would be a good time to update each other along the way. Willie was doing quite well with his government contracts. In fact, he was doing so well that he had gotten married and was raising his second family.

After making quick stops at government offices and meeting some of his associates, we headed for Uloma's flat in the local government area of Surulere. Uloma lived in one of the better areas of Surulere, in a cul-de-sac. As Willie came to a stop in front of the compound, I could see a house on the left and a duplex on the right. A security guard met us at the gate, and after telling him whom we wanted to see, we were directed to her upstairs flat. Apparently she had seen us coming through the front gate because she met us at the open door. We briefly embraced, and for a moment I was taken back to the first time we met.

I came back to reality when Willie said jokingly, "I'm here too."

Uloma offered refreshments, we both settled for a large cold beer, and for the next hour we talked about the current situation of the economy and how IBB's military regime was running the country. In between the general conversation, Uloma and I managed to get in a word or two about events leading up to our recent visit, and before leaving I gave her my address and a sincere promise to stay in touch.

After we left Uloma's flat, Willie wanted to check on the status of his permanent residence permit with an air force warrant officer by the name of George. Resident permits were more convenient than business and visitor visas because they only required renewing once a year instead of every three months. I never gave my visa status much thought because you had to be working for a Nigerian or foreign company or married to a Nigerian.

Military installations were a common sight in the Lagos residential areas. As we came to an air force security gate, Willie identified himself as a colonel, and the air force security guard snapped to attention and waved us in.

We waited in the reception office until George was informed of our arrival, and a few minutes later, a warrant officer came in with a big smile and said, "Good afternoon sir. Please follow me."

As we walked to his office, Willie introduced us, and I could tell George was happy to see another African American trying to do business in Nigeria. As we entered his office, he offered refreshments, but Willie said that we were just passing through and wanted to know if his resident permit was ready. George told him it was being delayed, but it should be ready in a couple of days, and he would bring the documents to Willie's house. In my brief conversation with George, I told him I might be interested in having his assistance in the near future and gave him my address. After our meeting, Willie dropped me off at the flat. I considered this one of my better days because I was able to connect with Uloma again and meet someone who could help with my visa status.

Three days later George dropped by in his Volkswagen and invited me out to have a beer in one of the better bukas. I accepted his offer, and while we were having a couple of beers, we were able to learn a bit about each other. George began by telling me that he was from a minority ethnic group in the eastern part of the country. He was about ten years younger than me and married, with a working wife and three wonderful children. He was a dedicated civil servant, and like most Nigerians, he was always looking for ways to supplement his income. As a civil servant, George depended on his clients' generosity and gratitude for his assistance because of his position. George asked the usual questions, but he was most curious to know why more African Americans were not taking advantage of the business opportunities in Nigeria, so I tried to explain the situation.

"The news from Africa is usually about drought, starvation, disease, civil war, military rule, dictatorships, and coups. When you consider all of these problems, it's no wonder there are only a few African Americans who are willing to leave their so-called comfortable lifestyles and put up with all of the challenges facing Nigeria."

"My dear brother, you are so correct. How can you invite somebody into our country when there is a good chance they will encounter all of our social, economical, and political problems? Right now foreigners come to Nigeria only for one thing, and that's business. Because of our problems, we can't take advantage of the tourist trade like Kenya and other African countries can. We are plagued by military rulers, coups, armed robbers, ethnic and religious problems, and the list goes on. It's a sad situation when you consider how the British forced us together. We have not had one day of unity and peace since Nigeria came into existence. Our leaders are corrupt because there is no accountability, and at times I feel we are destined to be this way because we have not achieved anything."

Like other Nigerians, George knew the problems of the country, and even though he was a career civil servant; he spoke his mind. I told him that it was unfortunate that African Americans and Africans had misconceptions of each other because of misinformation, disinformation, and lack of information. We ended our getting-acquainted conversation on a positive note as George dropped me off before going to check on one of his foreign clients on Victoria Island.

That evening, Pius, who was fast approaching forty, informed me that his bachelor days were coming to an end. This news meant that my days of sharing the flat were also ending. On such a short notice, I was fortunate to find a two-bedroom flat, which also came with a monthly lease agreement. Unfortunately, I spent very little time in my modest accommodations—because I was too busy driving Ms. Lucy. It was also during this time that I contracted malaria. It was like having the worst case of the flu with chills, fever, sweating, hallucinations, and a loss of appetite. With the help of chloroquine tablets, I was able to overcome the illness in three days. I would eventually contract malaria again before leaving Nigeria, but I still considered myself lucky to be in good health after living in the country for over fourteen years.

I gave up my new accommodations six months later, and it was also at this time that Lucy and I decided to end our relationship because we were only prolonging the inevitable. On the other hand, my relationship with Uloma had developed further, and in 1988 we decided it would be in our best interest to start living together. Moving in with Uloma without the traditional marriage ceremony was going to raise a few eyebrows among her family and friends, but we handled this minor crisis by assuring her parents that we would honor the traditional marriage custom later.

Uloma's spacious two-bedroom flat provided all of the basic amenities and a few luxuries, such as cable TV, phone service, and access to a generator. Needless to say, Uloma and I would still spend countless hours sitting on the balcony fighting off mosquitoes when we had no electricity and no fuel for the generator.

Uloma's younger brother Chidi was staying with her to pursue his education in Lagos because he, like other Nigerians migrating to Lagos, felt that he had a better chance of attending college, finding work, and starting his own business. He did not get admitted to the university because of a federal quota system that was designed to benefit the least Western-educated ethnic groups in the country, which were mainly in the north. Uloma was the eldest of her siblings and was expected to assist her younger siblings as much as possible. Chidi was finally able to start a wholesale clothing business with the help of Uloma and their father.

Uloma was sympathetic to my situation and suggested that we put what little resources we had together and try to make the best of it. Before I met Uloma in 1982, she had worked as a civil servant for the Nigerian National Petroleum Corporation, attended school in Britain, and been a public relations officer for an American consultant company in Lagos. Looking through her photo albums, I could see she had followed the latest fashion trends. Whenever Uloma traveled out of Nigeria, she, like the majority of Nigerian businesswomen, turned her trips into moneymaking ventures by always returning to Lagos with imported goods to sell to her waiting customers. Each day our commitment to each other became even stronger, which made it easier to set our goals, one of which was the completion of this manuscript.

Six months after moving in with Uloma, the two American cyclists Jesse and Ed were ready to start their West African cultural exchange bicycle tour. The cyclists visited universities and other learning institutions in each of the countries they traveled through. They took part in workshops and lectures with students who were also eager to exchange ideas and learn more about the visiting African Americans. Unfortunately, Ed fell ill from malaria somewhere between their starting point in Senegal and the Ivory Coast. Jesse was determined to make the trip alone, and although he would also contract malaria at the end of his trip, he was able to make it to Lagos. He contacted the U.S. Embassy there and was admitted to one of their local authorized hospitals. One of the nurses informed me that he was in the hospital, and upon visiting him, I was happy to see that he was regaining his strength. Two days later, he was discharged from the hospital, and he continued his recovery with us for two weeks before heading back to the United States. It was unfortunate that Jessie and Ed could not end their trip on a more positive note, but they were able to see parts of West Africa that very few foreigners had a chance to see, and their cultural exchange experiences with the people more than compensated for the discomforts of their trip.

Uloma's father paid us a visit because he had not yet met the man who was living with his daughter without the traditional wedding ceremony. I gave him a brief history of my experiences in Nigeria, how I met Uloma in 1982, and my financial situation. I also reassured him that we would have a traditional marriage ceremony soon. He was satisfied with my answer, but he also indicated that the Arochuka community could not recognize our union until the ceremony had been completed.

Because George was helping me with my legal status in the country, he would visit often, and on occasion he would ask me to ride along as he made his rounds. It was during one of these rides that I met Nando, the representative for Italy's largest military aircraft company, who was competing to win a contract from the Nigerian Air Force. Nando and I became good friends. Like most representatives, he was enjoying the perks that came with his position, which included housing, a driver, a cook, and servants. On this particular trip, Nando wanted George to help ease the formalities and escort some of his company officials who were coming into the country from Italy. While we were at Nando's, I met a Frenchman by the name of Jean. I thought nothing of the introduction other than that he was from France. Like the majority of foreigners, he was trying to cash in on the oil dollars by selling small arms to the armed forces and the national police.

Three weeks later, George came by and said he had some interesting news.

"Do you remember Jean, the Frenchman you met at Nando's?"

"Yes."

"I just finished talking with his secretary, and she told me that he left the country suddenly after men allegedly from the State Security Intelligence (SSI) paid him a visit a week ago. The SSI men said he was wanted for questioning regarding a possible fraud case. Jean tried to explain that he was not working for the company two years ago when the alleged fraud took place, but it was too late. The scam to rip him off was already in motion. He was blindfolded and taken by car to an undisclosed location in Lagos, and after arriving at the fake headquarters, the blindfold was removed, and Jean was once again informed of the charges."

George said by now Jean was shaking like a leaf until one of the men told him to relax and that the charges would probably be dropped if he could come up with some cash to placate the top bosses. Jean told them he could provide the cash and that he would not try to leave the country before coming up with the money. George had spoken with Jean's driver, who informed George that he and Jean had made several trips delivering cartons of undisclosed cash to the men in a one-week period. At that point, Jean decided it was in his best interest to leave the country as soon as possible, and he did so by crossing the land border and taking a flight from Benin's capital, Cotonou, to Paris. After hearing of the scam, I told George it was another unfortunate situation, and because there was no accountability, it was good chance of it happening again. He said, "This brings me to you. Before leaving the country, Jean asked his friend Nando for temporary assistance, who in turn asked me if I knew of anyone who could represent Jean. The security sample items were already in the country, and all that remains is a demonstration." The security items consisted of pop-up targets, and instructions on how to more efficiently train the Nigerian police and armed forces in handling small arms. My concern was that the scammers who got to Jean would come after me.

George said, "The possibilities of this happening are remote because coming back to the same company would only draw attention to them."

I told George I was interested, but I needed a couple of days to think about it.

I narrated the offer to Uloma, and we agreed that it would be a good opportunity, but that I should take caution because of the recent problems associated with the company. A week later I received correspondence from Jean, who was now living in South America, with special written instructions on how to proceed with the present office and the upcoming live demonstration Jean had lost a lot of money in the scam and could only provide ten thousand naira in working capital, but under the circumstances, George and I overlooked the much-needed financial support, hoping that we could still win the contract.

The following morning, I went to Jean's office. Like most foreign company buildings, it served also as his accommodations. His former Nigerian secretary, who introduced herself as Charlotte, met me at the front door. She gave me a tour of the two-bedroom flat with one of the rooms serving as an office. While she was explaining the office setup, the phone rang. Charlotte answered the call and began speaking in French.

The conversation lasted for about five minutes, and after hanging up, Charlotte said, "That was my boss in Lucerne, Switzerland. He has decided to close down the office."

This news was not surprising after hearing how Jean left the country. Charlotte was more disappointed than myself but said I could use the office, servants, cars, and driver for the next two weeks. This meant I would have to start operating from our flat and use public transportation, but I was already operating this way, so the adjustment was easy. The news from Charlotte's home office in Switzerland also meant that she would have to start looking for another source of employment. For the next two weeks, Charlotte and I worked together to prepare my first live demonstration of the security items for the police. I was impressed with Charlotte, who was of medium height, attractive, and ebony in complexion. After the demonstration, the police indicated a desire to purchase the new security items, but nothing ever came of it.

From the time I took over in 1989 until 1994, I would eventually coordinate three live security demonstrations, and after each demonstration, I would get the same promises but no orders. Having tried unsuccessfully to work with no operating funds, I decided to put the security items project on the back burner. Charlotte was able find employment at the Gabon Embassy, but her real desire was to get a job with the United Nations as a language translator. After wishing her success in her new endeavors, we parted ways. I lost contact with Charlotte about six months before leaving Nigeria, but I would stay in touch with George until the day I left.

Returning to the general situation, there was one segment of the society that caught my attention: the health sector. Even in the best of times, the general hospitals were no more than referral clinics. The private hospitals were better than the general hospitals, but the majority of Nigerians could not afford their services because of their high rates and unreasonable demands for deposits before providing service. This situation left the majority of Nigerians without any modern health care. Prior to the introduction of Western medicine, traditional doctors had been able to serve the people reasonably well; but times had changed, and some of the new diseases like AIDS rendered many of these traditional doctors helpless.

The health ministry tried to focus on primary health care to combat the deadlier illnesses. In the late 1960s and 1970s, it was estimated that more than one million Nigerians died annually from diarrhea, two hundred thousand children died annually or become permanently disabled from measles while polio and malaria claimed another one million lives. And on top of that, the country had the highest number of guinea worm patients in the world, cerebrospinal meningitis was widespread in the northern part of the country, and river blindness took a high toll on the rural population. The ministry of health's aim was to establish a solid health program for all by the year 2000.

The health ministry also tried to address the population problem with an awareness program called Mass Mobilization for Self-Reliance, Social Justice, and Economic Recovery (MAMSER). The MAMSER program was a creation of the IBB regime. It was intended to help motivate people to support their social programs. With this in mind, the government introduced the Family Planning Program. But the government made a mistake initially by saying that women should not have more than four children without putting any of the responsibility on the men. The women strongly rejected this, arguing that men were the cause of the population problems because they could marry more than one wife. The government had some success in alleviating this program, mainly due to the harsh economic realities of the country.

The economy was biting down hard on the average Nigerian, and it was only continuing to get worse. The IBB regime tried to soften the blow of the SAP by introducing a number of relief programs for Nigerians at the lower end of the economic scale. One of the more popular relief packages was the People's Bank, which was designed to provide loans, ranging from fifty naira to two thousand naira, to the less privileged. The People's Bank was initially well received because many Nigerians could not obtain loans from the conventional banking system. But shortly after the bank was launched in October 1989, it encountered serious fraud problems in some of its local branches. This left the People's Bank with a credibility problem, and within a short time it closed.

On the political scene, the Armed Forces Ruling Council establish two political parties. One party, called the Social Democratic Party (SDP), leaned slightly to the left while the other party, the National Republican Convention (NRC), was a little to the right. While IBB was trying to institute this two party political system, he received an early-morning wake-up call from coup leader Major Orkar and his compatriots. IBB was able to escape but his military aid was killed in the early-morning shoot-out. Usually, within hours after a coup, there would be an announcement of who had won control of the country. But in this case, nobody knew the outcome of the shoot-out because there were two different announcements. The first announcement came from the coup plotters. After formally introducing himself over the radio, the new leader gave a host of reasons for why they overthrew the IBB regime, "We wish to emphasize that this is not just another coup but a well-conceived and well-executed revolution of the marginalized, oppressed, and enslaved peoples of the middle belt and the south with a goal of freeing ourselves and our children, yet unborn, from internal slavery and colonization by a clique in this country."

Three hours later, however, the IBB regime came on the radio with an announcement that the dissident coup plotters had been wiped out. The military regime arrested most of the conspirators, and after a speedy military trial on April 30, 1990, some were placed before a firing squad while others received various jail terms. The Nigerian people had once again experienced another military action over which they had no control. Having now survived two coup attempts, IBB sped up the plans of moving the federal capital from Lagos to Abuja.

Nigeria's economic situation still continued to worsen. In 1989, IBB and his financial advisers thought they could solve some of the country's financial woes by deregulating the banking sector, but this only led to more problems. Some new banks, finance houses, and the more popular "miracle banks" took undue advantage of the loopholes and the lack of liability in the new banking system. Most of these new financial institutions were able to start their new operations without showing their real net worth. This situation allowed unqualified people to operate with reckless abandon. This was the case with the "miracle" finance houses, which offered up to 60 percent on deposits of thirty to ninety days. Amazingly, these financial institutions were attracting not only private citizens but banks and government agencies as well. Some of the investors would divert funds from their department's account with the hope that they could personally collect the interest before returning the funds. One unfortunate depositor used funds from his church to cash in on the unbelievable interest rates, and he ended up losing everything. He was so upset that he tried to burn down the finance office, but the surrounding neighbors, in fear that their nearby houses would also go up in flames, persuaded him not to set the building ablaze. Fortunately for Nigerians, the new banks disappeared as fast as they appeared but not before causing financial losses for the majority of the depositors.

In 1993 while I was researching material for this manuscript in our flat, the security guard informed me that a gentleman wanted to see me at the front gate. From the living room window, I could see a man standing by a car. I assumed he was Nigerian, but upon reaching the gate, I was still unable to recognize this person who apparently knew me.

We looked at each other in silence until he said, "You don't know me?"

I gave him a concentrated look, and it dawned on me that it was my cousin from Michigan.

Before I could say his name, he said, "I'm Robert, your first cousin."

This was my first time seeing Robert, and I asked him to forgive my ignorance for not recognizing him. We greeted each other for the first time, and after he introduced his wife, we made our way back upstairs.

Robert said their Michigan business group had been in the country for almost a week, but he had not had an opportunity to reach me until now. I asked Robert about the product he was trying to sell in Nigeria, and he told me that his company produced water-based chemicals used in cleaning oil stains from airport tarmacs, oil rigs, platforms, etc. Robert had a good product, but I had to let him know that his product was only as good as his contact. The people running the country at that time were the Hausas in the north, and the leader of his business group was an Ibo from the east.

Robert gave me the impression that he was basically aware of how business was done in Nigeria, so I decided to let it rest for the time being. Before leaving, Robert wanted to know if I could come by the hotel the next morning and pick up a package of personal items he had brought from the United States.

That evening I told Uloma of the visit I had with Robert and his wife and that they were returning to the United States in two days. Unfortunately, she would not have the opportunity to meet them because of conflicting schedules. The next morning, I headed for my former hotel on Victoria Island, and it brought back memories of missed opportunities. Upon reaching their room, I met Robert and his wife preparing to have breakfast in the restaurant. Robert suggested we step out on the balcony to give his wife more privacy and us a chance to talk. As we looked out over the swimming pool, I began to tell Robert that the opportunities were boundless in Nigeria, but the abundant problems made business difficult. I briefly told him about military rule, corruption, and the northern region dominance of the country. It was Robert's wife tap on the window to let him know that she was ready, and it brought our conversation to an end. Before we headed out to our different destinations, Robert indicated that if I should find an organization interested in his product, he would be willing to work with me. I wished I had better news for Robert, but outside of the expense he and his wife had incurred in coming to Nigeria, their losses were small in comparison to what I had experienced. Robert and his wife left for the United States the next day with only promises that his business trip would bring him government contracts.

Even though the strike was over, the general situation continued to deteriorate. Between Uloma and me, the armed forces contracts had dwindle to nothing, and the local business contracts were rare. With each Nigerian crisis, I was putting more time into the manuscript. When I first told Uloma that I was writing about my Nigerian experiences, she had reservations because some foreign and Nigerian writers had portrayed the country in a negative way without offering any constructive criticism. But after explaining that I would write constructively, she offered her full support.

IBB wanted to reassure his critics that he was determined to leave the seat of power on August 27, 1993, and he handed over the government to a twenty-seven-member Civilian Transition Council that would take over in December 1993. The council members were prominent Nigerians, including the former chairman of the United African Company (UAC), Chief Ernest Shonekan.

While IBB was trying to convince Nigerians that he was not running the country, his manufactured two-party system was somehow able to take hold and select presidential candidates. Chief Abiola of the Social Democratic Party (SDP) and Alhaji Tofa of the National Republican Convention (NRC) would run for president, but there was controversy. During the SDP convention, the northern elite successfully persuaded Chief Abiola to accept a northern Muslim running mate. Usually, any candidate running for the office of president would select a vice president from a religious faith other than his or her own. In this case, Chief Abiola, who was also Muslim, should have chosen a Christian running mate. But the Christian voters were so disillusioned with the military that they were willing to overlook the fact that this pair represented only one religion.

Chief Abiola was one of Nigeria's wealthiest men, having come from humble beginnings only to become one of the world's top international businessmen through his use of government contracts. His break came while he was working for International Telephone Telegraph (ITT) as a controller. The federal government owed the company a large debt, and Abiola was instrumental in recovering the money. For this, he was named the company's chairman in Nigeria and its vice president for Africa and the Middle East. In 1974, he started his own communications company. He became involved in other business interests, which included banking, air transportation, shipping, publishing, oil prospecting, agriculture, and entertainment. A noted philanthropist, he had donated large sums to education, sports, and numerous social and political causes. He called for reparations from the western countries to compensate African peoples for the transatlantic slave trade. He had at least five wives and had fathered at least forty children.

Members of the international community, including the United States, were on hand to ensure that the elections went off without a hitch. With all the suspicion and distrust IBB had generated among many Nigerians, it was surprising that he actually allowed the candidates of the two government-sponsored parties to campaign. Amid the suspicion surrounding IBB's transition to a civilian-rule government, a nongovernmental organization, the Association for Better Nigeria (ABN), was established to promote the retention of the IBB regime. The ABN stated that because of the country's current situation, it would not be in Nigeria's best interest to elect a civilian government. It was rumored that IBB was covertly supporting the ABN because there was never an open attempt to stop the ABN from campaigning for their cause.

Two days prior to the much-awaited presidential elections, the ABN got an Abuja High Court injunction to stop the elections, but the government Electoral Commission (NEC) set by the IBB regime and headed by an Ibo defied the court ruling and asked Nigerians to turn out and vote on Saturday, June 12, 1993. Some of the confused voters stayed away from the polls because of conflicting reports, but for those who voted, the majority stated that it was the fairest election the country had ever had.

Halfway through the voting, and with Chief Abiola clearly in the lead, a chief judge from the north issued an order restraining the NEC from announcing the voting results. Condemnation came from all quarters. The United States reacted swiftly by expelling all Nigerian armed forces personnel and their families from the United States and barring any future military and senior civilian personnel and their families from traveling to the United States. The British government made limited restrictions on the Nigerian military as well. On June 23, 1993, the federal military government of IBB annulled the June 12 elections.

Chief Abiola, now fearing that his life was threatened because of the annulled elections, fled the country in his private jet. He landed in Britain in the early hours of the morning and held a hastily arranged press conference stating that he was seeking Britain's support for additional sanctions against the IBB government for annulling the elections and for not releasing the results. The British had already placed limited sanctions against Nigeria and felt there was not much more they could do but urge the Nigerian military government to return to democratic rule as soon as possible. From Britain, Chief Abiola traveled to the United States, where the reception was also lukewarm.

Another notable event in June 1993 was the arrest of Ken Saro-Wiwa. This well known author, poet, teacher, TV scriptwriter, dramatist, and social activist was arrested on frivolous charges by the IBB regime. Saro-Wiwa's arrest was an attempt by IBB to suppress any and all agitation coming from the oil-producing areas in the midwestern and eastern parts of the country. Saro-Wiwa, who was from the Ogoni ethnic group, was the first to protest openly about the unjust conditions being perpetrated against the Ogonis. He would eventually spend over a month in several horrendous detention centers in the Port Harcourt prison.

Fortunately, I have never had the opportunity of being an involuntary guest in a Nigerian police cell, but the stories I have heard are ghastly beyond description. The overcrowding of cells contributed to a number of unnecessary deaths. The detainees complained of hunger, and unsanitary conditions added to their health problems. There was also the problem of diseases like scabies and typhoid fever, and splash baths were almost nonexistent. If you were a newcomer, the hardened criminals would charge fees for your involuntary lodging; and if you happened to be broke, they would force you to do unsanitary chores like carrying the latrine bucket and standing up all night fanning mosquitoes away from other cell members.

IBB's Transitional Council was continuing to meet strong opposition from within and outside the government. This forced IBB to establish another temporary civilian government called the Interim National Government (ING), which was also headed by Chief Shonekan. On August 27, 1993, IBB voluntarily abdicated his position of power as promised.

A month later, Chief Abiola returned to the country to try and claim his mandate to become Nigeria's president, but this turned out to be a mistake. To make matters worse, he would never see his freedom again. To make matters worse, General Abacha and two of his closest military aides entered the temporary presidential office of Chief Shonekan and requested that he resign his position as head of the Interim National Government on November 17, 1993. The reason Abacha gave for taking over the country was because Shonekan did not have the respect and support needed to operate the government. Nigerian leadership was once again on shaky grounds; the current crisis surrounding the annulled June 12 elections, and the threat of another civil war made it easy for General Abacha to take over the government.

In November of 1993, while Abacha was taking over the country, Uloma and I were quietly married in the civil courts. As we were enjoying our new legal status as husband and wife and preparing for our move to the United States, Chief Abiola was watching his grasp on Nigeria's presidency slip away. He became desperate and stepped up his campaign against the Abacha regime; his former running mate revealed that he and other prominent Nigerians had invited the military to take over from the Interim National Government.

Chief Abiola tried to deny this, but word slipped out that he had sent a controversial letter to negotiate peace and friendship with the former military head of state, IBB. Once again, Chief Abiola tried to make amends by publicly asking Nigerians, through some of the daily newspapers, to forgive him. It was rumored that Chief Abiola's visit to General Abacha after his takeover from the Interim National Government was to ensure that his former party members were included in Abacha's cabinet. Abiola hoped that Abacha would install him as president because of the annulled June 12 elections.

General Abacha was not new to Nigerian military politics, and he was impatiently waiting in the wings for any opportunity to carry out his plan to take control of the country's treasury. Unlike his military predecessor, Abacha ruled the country in seclusion; and when he did appear in public, he was seldom seen without his dark glasses. Abacha was not going to tolerate any civilian confrontation, so he dismantled the Interim National Government, ending the transition to civilian rule started by IBB.

Nigerians had cheered when the military took over from the Shagari civilian government, and they had cheered when IBB took over from Buhari. But nobody cheered for Abacha when he orchestrated his palace coup and eliminated civilian rule. Abacha's first step was to try and defuse tensions surrounding the June 12 elections while introducing another unnecessary constitutional conference. His next step was to end any support for Chief Abiola. He accomplished this by offering plum government positions to some of Abiola's closest supporters.

In May 1994, Chief Abiola increased his demands to become Nigeria's civilian president by declaring that he would become president on the anniversary of the annulled 1993 elections. Around this time, General Abacha felt it was time to make his move on Chief Abiola, and he placed him under house arrest. Somehow, Chief Abiola was able or allowed to escape and gave several public speeches over the next two weeks in Lagos. General Abacha had lost what little patience he had left, and he had Abiola rearrested and flown to an unknown destination in the north and thrown into detention.

In an effort to deceive Nigerians, Abacha suggested a national constitutional conference. The constitution was not Nigeria's real problem; it was common knowledge that amendments were used to make changes. But Abacha was looking for time and reviewing the entire constitution would give him at least one year of control over the country's treasury. The constitutional conference took place during turbulent times. Tensions were high, the present leadership was on shaky grounds, the economic situation continued sliding in the wrong direction, and inflation was running out of control. There was also civil unrest and the threat of even more strikes from the hospitals, universities, and other learning institutions. The country was facing high unemployment, crime was rampant, international fraud had reached new heights, and assassins felt as though they had the authority to kill. Unfortunately, the delegates at the conference did not deliberate on any of these pressing social issues.

The lifeline of the Nigerian economy was cut off when the Nigerian Union of Petroleum and Natural Gas Workers officially went on strike on July 5, 1994. The strike hit the Abacha regime where it really hurt. They were now losing oil revenues, which meant less money for Abacha's treasury. In an effort to beat the strike, Abacha directed the army to start lifting and transporting fuel to the filling stations, but this had very little impact on the problem because the army could not operate the refineries. The government-owned company in charge of Nigeria's oil industry, the Nigerian National Petroleum Corporation (NNPC), suffered from the same problems as the other state-owned companies. The NNPC operated four refineries; and none of them had ever operated at full capacity due to neglect, old age, poor maintenance, frequent shutdowns, and the lack of accountability. Nigeria is now the leading crude oil producer in Africa and the fourth leading supplier of crude oil to the United States. Unfortunately, it imports 40 to 60 percent of the refined oil products for local use.

The situation in Nigeria had drawn the concerns of the U.S. president Clinton who asked Rev. Jesse Jackson to lead a delegation to Nigeria to discuss the current unrest, Chief Abiola's continued detention, and the government's commitment toward democracy. The U.S. delegation arrived in Nigeria in July of 1994 under strong criticism from Mr. Osahon, the leader of the Pan African Movement in Nigeria. The Pan African leader insisted that the American civil rights campaigner never possessed the needed credibility for the present task. He also stated that Reverend Jackson had never been on the side of truth in any issue affecting the African continent and that he represented the interests of the white elite.

He further stated that Reverend Jackson did not represent the black movement or interests in the United States and that currently the most influential black leader in the United States was Minister Louis Farrakhan. No one can dispute Minister Farrakhan's achievements for African Americans, but he and the Nation of Islam were perceived by white mainstream America as a separatist and radical organization. This made it difficult, if not impossible, for the U.S. government to use him as an envoy. It was not Reverend Jackson's fault that every time he came to Nigeria, it was going through another unnecessary crisis. With all due respect to President Clinton, Minister Farrakhan, Reverend Jackson, and the Pan African leader, it would not have made any difference who the United States sent as an envoy because there simply could not be any success under the dictatorial rule of General Abacha.

After Reverend Jackson held separate talks with Abacha and Abiola, he expressed concerns that the United States should try to intervene as a mediator. He also felt that Nigeria was on the verge of entering another civil war on the same scale as Rwanda or even worse. I felt the time to have intervened was during the 1914 amalgamation or perhaps the country's independence in 1960 or after the tragic civil war in 1967 or any of the numerous crises from that period until now.

The ongoing strike had made water less accessible, and the scarcity of fuel had turned many people into illegal petroleum dealers. We adjusted to the shortage by using less water, and in regards to petroleum products, our major concern was the lack of diesel fuel for the generator. Without electricity, we had to deal with several problems, from mosquitoes to spoiled food. To protect ourselves from the malaria-carrying mosquitoes, we would fan ourselves in the evening and night hours until we had electricity or until our arms became tired. We adjusted to the shortage of gas by cooking less, and to keep the food from spoiling, we would reheat it at night and in the morning.

The fuel shortage had become so severe that some Lagos residents were using firewood to cook their meals, a fire hazard which led to injuries and deaths. Prior to the strike, the price for gasoline was around three naira per liter, and now it was selling for between sixty and seventy naira. In addition, some unscrupulous individuals were selling adulterated gasoline and kerosene in an effort to increase their profits. As a result, there was often news of someone being seriously burnt or killed when their kerosene stove or lantern exploded.

It was during this time that I had the misfortune of becoming ill. This was yet another sign that I would have to start seriously thinking about returning to the United States since my health was more important than my desire to do business in Nigeria. This particular sickness began with everyone in our household getting headaches though we could not figure out the cause. A week later, we were finally able to trace the cause of our headaches to the leaking gas cylinder, but by that time my headaches had become worse, and three mornings later I awakened with only half vision in my left eye. Fearful that I might lose the rest of my left eyesight, Uloma took me to a nearby optometrist. During the medical check-in they noticed that my blood pressure was high, and the eye doctor suggested that I see a medical doctor. The reputation of the Lagos general hospitals was not very encouraging, so we decided to visit a private doctor. Upon reaching the private medical clinic, the doctor informed me that my blood pressure was 213. He also indicated that the problem with my eye was the result of a mild stroke and that it would be in my best interest to check into the hospital immediately.

After staying in the hospital for two days, I was impressed with their services. They managed to lower my blood pressure and restore full vision to my left eye. I felt good enough to leave, but the doctor insisted that I stay another day for further observation. Unknown to me, the doctor, who was also part owner of the private hospital, was holding me because of my unpaid medical bill. That following afternoon, Uloma arrived, and I explained to her that I was ready to leave, but the doctor wanted me to stay another day for further observation. She told me that she was aware of the problem and that she knew the real reason for keeping me in the hospital.

She told me, "The medical bill was more than I expected, and I didn't want to tell you because of your condition. Since that time, I was able to come up with the balance, and we are free to go."

As we left, I thanked the doctor for the treatment, and I also let him know that I was disappointed in their method of collecting payments.

On August 4, 1994, the Nigerian labor unions called off their strike and gave up on the possibility of Chief Abiola's release from detention. It was unfortunate that Chief Abiola and other political detainees were still in confinement, and the general situation in the country had only become worse.

Perhaps the most heated debate at the conference was whether the states or the federal government should have control of the natural resources. The northern states did not favor the states controlling their own resources because they felt it would endanger the so-called unity of the country. Another reason they were in favor of government control was that they were benefiting from the process of relying on the resources and revenues of a region other than their own. Prior to the rapid decrease in revenue sharing in Nigeria (1960-1967), the four major regions received 50 percent of the natural resources generated in their different regions. Since that time, successive military and civilian governments continued the decreases in revenues to the regions, especially the eastern and midwestern regions. This process began with Lieutenant Colonel Gowon, who decreased revenues by 5 percent in 1970. Next up was General Obasanjo, who in 1977 decrease revenues by 20 percent. Next was Shagari, who cut back another 20 percent in 1981. General Buhari removed three and a half percent, leaving one and half percent for the states from the original 50 percent.

Before the pointless constitutional delegation ended on October 25, 1994, it voted to allow the federal government to keep control of the country's minerals, including oil and natural gas. This decision did nothing to encourage other states to revitalize and explore revenue sources in their own areas. The delegates also decided to keep a strong central government despite requests from the southern regions that wanted more regional control. The delegates also agreed to give the oil-producing areas only 13 percent of the oil revenue allocation collectively. It was nothing close to the 50 percent they were asking for, and once again, the minorities in the south had lost out in their bid to have a stronger and larger share of the revenues derived from resources coming from their land.

Returning to the general situation in Nigeria, there was another area affected by the unrest in the country: the educational system. Nigerian university employees embarked on an indefinite strike to protest, among other things, the continued detention of Chief Abiola and to support the immediate termination of military rule. In the past, Nigeria had prided itself on its educational system, but since the early 1980s, its academic institutions had diminished to the point of major concern. University students attributed the deteriorating conditions to frequent closures of universities from employee strikes, which led to a mass exodus of seasoned teachers and a general lack of concern from the federal government. This intellectual brain drain left the system and facilities in complete disarray.

Chapter Six

A Government on the Ropes

In March of 1995, an American hit the front pages of many daily Nigerian newspapers, but this time it was not the United States making news. The TransAfrica Organization, headed by Mr. Randall Robinson, wanted a U.S. embargo on Nigeria. He went on to say that it was possible to affect a boycott of an international nature just as it was done against the former racist government of South Africa. Regarding criticism of his organization for targeting an African country, Robinson explained, "It is not easy to publicly criticize black leadership. It is uncomfortable and disquieting. But we are left with no alternative. We will oppose the Nigerian military government with as much tenacity as we opposed the military regime in Haiti." Nigerians did not welcome further sanctions, but they did appreciate Mr. Robinson's concerns about returning the country to civilian rule.

Also in March 1995, General Abacha arrested two retired military generals, one of whom was General Obasanjo, a Yoruba and the former military head of state. No reason was given for the arrest, but it concerned the Yorubas because Chief Abiola was already in detention. This prompted yet another protest from the international community against the Abacha military regime, but as long as these concerns did not interfere with Abacha's ability to loot the treasury, their concerns fell on deaf ears.

International leaders continued to press Abacha to set democratic reforms in place. Former president Jimmy Carter and his wife arrived in the country in March 1995 to review his Global 2000 program, which was designed to eradicate guinea worm and river blindness worldwide. It is important to note that in 1978, President Carter was the first American president to have visited Nigeria; and at that time, General Obasanjo was the military head of state. While President Carter was in the country, he made a courtesy call on General Abacha, and the highlight of his visit was speaking on behalf of the political detainees, especially General Obasanjo, who he described as an international figure and friend.

President Carter's visit with Abacha was not enough to keep the dictator from announcing in April 1995 that his regime was holding General Obasanjo under house arrest and General Yar'Adua in detention due to implications in an alleged coup attempt. The majority of Nigerians felt Abacha had fabricated the coup attempt to suppress opposition. The two generals were tried under charges of "concealing treason," which meant they were accused of knowing about a planned coup and did nothing to stop it. The military tribunal sentenced them to death by firing squad, along with about forty other people implicated in the alleged coup. After constant pressure from the international community, Abacha reduced General Obasanjo's sentence from life to fifteen years, and Yar'Adua's from death to twenty-five years. The others, including Chris Anyanwu a woman journalist, received prison terms ranging from six months to two years.

Fear once again reigned supreme for the Ibos living in the northern state of Kano.

A satanic pamphlet went into circulation in June 1995, stating, "This is to inform you that it is in your best interest and life security to pack out of Kano City with immediate effect; otherwise, your lives will be in danger."

With past religious disturbances, it didn't take long for Ibos and other non-Muslims to start heading south. It's important to note that Islam does not teach or condone this type of behavior. The Muslim radicals were small in number but influential enough to incite other Muslims to carry out acts of terror, destruction, and death.

Returning to my situation, I unwittingly took part in an oil deal that turned out to be a scam. It all started when my friend Willie told me that he was assisting a group of financial investors from the United States who had been successful in closing an oil deal with the Nigerian National Petroleum Corporation (NNPC). I told Willie that I had been talking with a Nigerian medical doctor, whom I met through a mutual Nigerian friend, and he indicated that he had access to a shipload of oil. Willie, feeling confident because their group had just signed an oil deal the day before, agreed to meet the doctor the following day in his associate's room at the Eko Holiday Inn hotel.

The next day, Willie and I went to Victoria Island and met Ron, his business associate from America. A short while later, the doctor arrived and explained that he had strong connections with the NNPC and that he had an allocation for oil. The oil allocation was issued to a U.S. company, but because of a technicality, the U.S. company could no longer complete the oil deal. Willie and I had already agreed to share the broker's fees, and everything was moving along smoothly until Willie asked whose name was on the contract.

The doctor, thinking he had a sure deal, said, "As you can see, this contract was just signed two days ago."

Willie skimmed through the documents, then said he had to run down to the lobby for a minute; but before leaving, he handed the documents to Ron. I wondered why Willie had to leave suddenly, and I waited for Ron's response. After reading the documents, Ron asked me to follow him to the balcony. He told me the reason Willie had left the room was that the doctor was trying to sell them their own oil allocation. When we informed the doctor that his scam had been exposed, he embarrassingly went into a mild shock. We advised the doctor to leave the hotel as soon as possible because there was a good chance Willie was trying to contact the police. The doctor wasted no time leaving the room. This was my last attempt to help broker a shipload of oil.

Returning to my situation in the United States, I had not heard anything from Mr. Grant for over two months until one evening Uloma and I were recapping the day's events in August of 1995. She informed me that Mr. Grant had died of a heart attack two months earlier. Her main reason for not telling me at the time was because I was recovering from a mild stroke as a result of high blood pressure. I was faced with yet another personal crisis, and after several conversations with Uloma, she convinced me that it would be better if I momentarily forget about business in Nigeria and return to the United States. If I had any doubts about leaving the country, the death of Mr. Grant dispelled my hesitation. As I took in the news of his passing, highlights of Mr. Grant's life raced through my mind. It began with his teaching and coaching career in 1952 at John Muir Elementary School and the Alameda Recreational Department. He later taught American and black history at Encinal High School, which included coaching football and track. He also managed to find time to work as a businessman. The number of athletes and students who came under his tutelage are too numerous to mention but some of the more popular included Bill Russell, K. C. Jones, Willie Stargell, Tommy Harper, Curt Motton, and Mac Arthur Lane.

After the news of Mr. Grant's death, I decided to concentrate on returning to the United States, all the while hoping I could still get a contract that would make the time I spent in Nigeria worthwhile. I started making plans to leave by December, and Uloma would follow a couple of months later. The second part of the plan was to prepare myself to reenter the job market after being self-employed for almost twenty years.

One evening while Uloma and I were watching the evening news, the newscaster caught our attention when she said that Gen. Colin Powell had allegedly stated during an interview with the *New Yorker* magazine (September 25, 1995) that Nigerians as a group are dishonest people. We were shocked to hear this reported statement coming from an African American who had reached the top of his profession and who was even more respected as a result of the Gulf War in 1991.

Abacha's information officer said, "The Nigerian government regarded General Powell as an international figure and was, therefore, closely studying the disparaging statements on Nigeria credited to him."

The Congress of Nigerians Abroad, which described the attack as irresponsible, stated, "It is becoming fashionable for opportunists of all hues to engage in mindless generalization when they talk about Nigeria and Nigerians."

They called for Nigerians abroad to unite and strongly condemn General Powell's negative remarks.

The Organization of Nigerian Professionals said, "It was regrettable that instead of assisting Nigeria in its present efforts, brothers like Powell are bent on finishing the country. It hurts that Nigeria has become everybody's football."

My first thought was that this couldn't be the same General Powell who not only visited Nigeria on a goodwill tour but also invited General Abacha to Washington DC to receive one of the highest military honors. Unfortunately, it was no secret that Nigeria had gained more than its share of negative attention from international scams like 419 (advance fee fraud) and drug trafficking, but it was also obvious that the majority of Nigerians were not involved in these criminal activities.

A month later, General Powell apologized to Nigerians by saying, "I deeply regret and apologize for the distress this has caused in the Nigerian community. I have the greatest respect for the people of Nigeria. I was venting my frustration over the lack of progress toward democracy in Nigeria and the impact of corruption on the part of some Nigerians in their country. Unfortunately, my comments in the context of the article gave the impression that I was disparaging all Nigerians; nothing could be further from the truth. I have steadfastly supported the desire of the Nigerian people to live under civilian democratic rule. I will continue to seek every opportunity to speak out for democracy in Nigeria."

Nigeria and other African countries need constructive criticism and not stories requiring this type of an apology especially coming from an African American leader.

As for Saro-Wiwa, he was arrested again by the military government in May 1994 for the murder of four of his kinsmen. He and eight other members of the Ogoni ethnic group were found guilty and sentenced to death by hanging on October 31, 1995. People with good conscience were shocked after hearing the verdict. The sad part about this kangaroo trial was that their only crime was fighting for the basic human rights of their people. Saro-Wiwa's final words to the special military tribunal after being sentenced were the following:

> My lord, I was adjudged guilty before I was charged. Even during the trial, I had been adjudged guilty. Fifteen months ago, government officials told the international community that I was guilty. In the course of this trial, I have been brutalized and my family almost ruined. In and out of prison, my ideas would live. I am happy this

country has benefited from the ideas of MOSOP. Shell has started doing what MOSOP demanded. Secondly, the matter of ethnic minority has been accepted. We in MOSOP have made a very wonderful contribution to the development of our fatherland. Ogoni people have suffered tremendously, and our plea is that the suffering must stop.

At this point, Saro-Wiwa's plea was cut off by the tribunal chairman, asking Saro-Wiwa not to reopen the case through his plea. Nigerians and the rest of the world were expecting Abacha to step in at the last minute and reduce the death sentences, but on November 10, 1995, his regime carried out the executions in blatant disregard of national and international pleas for clemency.

To get a better understanding of Saro-Wiwa and the Ogoni crisis, I think it's best to go back to 1957 when Shell and British Petroleum were awarded the total land areas of Nigeria for oil exploration. In Nigeria's haste to reap the benefits of this precious commodity, they ignored the welfare of the people and the natural environment. This blatant disregard allowed the environment and social fabric to deteriorate while the oil companies and some of the leaders in the Nigerian government collected huge profits. In the meantime, the affected people suffered from gas flares, oil spills, laying of pipelines through farm lands, polluted rivers, and other damages caused from oil drilling without taking the proper precautions.

It was truly unfortunate that four Ogoni leaders were killed, and it was even more tragic that the Abacha regime roped in nine more Ogoni leaders by accusing them of murdering the first four. The Ogoni community lost a total of thirteen leaders, and only God knows how many other members of this small oil-rich community had lost their lives simply for addressing the problems of human rights violations of their people to the government and oil companies.

On the day of the executions, sources from within the prison stated that Saro-Wiwa and the other condemned men had no idea that they were going to be executed that day as they sat on a long bench in a room next door to the execution room. The first person called was Saro-Wiwa, and after entering the execution room, he knew why they were all sitting there. The warrant for his death was read aloud, which was a recap of the fabricated events that had brought him and the others to this point. The hangman dropped a hood over his head, and with the noose firmly around Saro-Wiwa's neck, another hangman drew the pulley downward, but the trap door failed to open. They tried again and again, but nothing happened, and they returned Saro-Wiwa to the bench. This was when he told the others that in the next room was the execution chamber. After hearing the news, some of the men broke down.

The death call came once again, but this time they called for one of Saro-Wiwa's compatriots, and the pulley worked with precision. It appeared the hangmen wanted to get Saro-Wiwa out of the way as soon as possible because they called him back in after his compatriot had become a victim to the noose. The pulley failed to work once again, and like before he was returned to the bench as the number of men on the bench dwindled. Once again, Saro-Wiwa was sent into the room of death, and the pulley once again failed to activate. This was the third time Saro-Wiwa had defied the gallows, and the executioners must have wondered why the pulley worked for others and not for Saro-Wiwa.

Perhaps the mental agonies of seeing his compatriots enter the execution chamber, never to return, was more tormenting than the mechanism failing each time they tried to hang him. So Saro-Wiwa, after watching his compatriots die by the hangman's noose, prayed for the end to come.

Moments before he was finally hanged, he asked his persecutors one last question, "What kind of country is this that kills those fighting for a better life for their people?"

The Abacha regime was not only heartless before, during, and after the supposed trial but also after the execution. The men were quickly buried in a mass grave, and acid was poured over their bodies for fast decomposition. They even placed tight security around the gravesite to make sure the relations could not exhume the bodies in order to give them a proper burial. It was a sad day in Nigeria. After hearing news of the executions, the only thing the people could do was mourn in silence. The British Commonwealth reacted first by suspending the Nigerian delegation not only from their conference in New Zealand but from the Commonwealth organization as well. President Mandela led the way for Africa by recalling South Africa's high commissioner to Nigeria. The U.S. permanent representative at the United Nations, Madeline Albright, said in part that the U.S. government deplored the executions and that the United States would continue to oppose IMF loans, credits, and debt relief for Nigeria. The next possible line of U.S. action could include sanctions on Nigeria's oil output of which U.S. imports were about 44 percent. But the oil sanctions against Nigeria were highly unlikely because the United States already had sanctions against Iran, Iraq, and Libya.

Shell's response to the Ogoni crisis was too late and too little because after more than thirty years of flaring gas, accidental oil spills, and other related problems in drilling for oil, it had left the oil- and gas-producing areas devastated. The director of Shell's operation in Nigeria, Mr. Anderson said that Shell does not interfere in the political issues of a country, but it became indirectly involved when it became part of a joint venture in the Nigerian oil industry. The director said Shell was spending more than one hundred million dollars on environmental programs, but the late Saro-Wiwa estimated that Shell and the past governments have taken nothing less than ninety-six billion dollars from Ogoni land since they first began exporting oil in the late 1950s. One hundred million dollars to the oil-producing areas was certainly a step in the right direction, but it was a drop in the bucket compared to the oil they had already taken, not to mention the lack of environmental concern and controls. This tragic situation could have been avoided if Shell and the Nigerian government had taken the appropriate steps to ensure that the mineral producing areas were compensated from the time they first struck oil. It's unfortunate that this "tragic union" forged by the British has brought nothing but untold suffering for the people of Nigeria, and their latest victims were the Ogoni community.

My Nigerian Odyssey was finally coming to an end, and after learning how Nigeria was brought together by the British, and how the country got it's name, I devoted the remainder of my time to the manuscript. I made a point to expose these concerns after witnessing the unnecessary suffering that Nigerians had to go through on a daily basis. I hope that by writing about my experiences in Nigeria I can help bring some positive changes to the major ethnic groups and minorities as well.

Though I had witnessed host of unnecessary disappointments in Nigeria, I had also experienced some wonderful times, and certainly meeting my wife was one of the most memorable moments. I tried to cover as many events and individuals as possible, and for those who were not mentioned, please do not feel offended because you are also in my thoughts. With a heavy heart, and a strong desire to write about my Nigerian experiences, I received my wife's blessings and left Nigeria on December 22, 1995.

After Notes

1996-2007

Upon returning home, I had a number of things to do, and the first was getting a medical checkup. I was able to accomplish this through the Veterans Administration. I was also able to stay with a relative temporarily, and found permanent housing shortly after my wife's arrival in April 1996.

I was able to reenter the job market without too much difficulty after being self-employed for over eighteen years. I concentrated on part-time jobs to allow myself time to work on the manuscript. My jobs included working as a U.S postal clerk, juvenile group councilor, recreational facilities specialist, and a job that included delivering meals on wheels. My wife supported our mission by working as an administration assistant and subsequently as a part-time medical unit assistant. My main objective was to get the book published, and I knew that without any prior writing experience this task was going to be very difficult. However, my determination to get the story out was far greater than the difficulties.

For the next ten years, we stayed in touch with friends and acquaintances in Nigeria through phone calls, letters, e-mails, local social events, and my wife's visits to the country. We received visits from my wife's mother and other relatives when they came to America. Unfortunately, they all expressed the same feelings that any hope for Nigeria under its present condition was fading fast.

Since we left Nigeria, a number of events have occurred that are worth mentioning. One particular event of importance was the passing of Dr. Nanamdi Azikiwe (Zik) in May 1996. In a way, he shared something with the other Nigerian leaders that had passed before him; he died without ever seeing peace and unity in *A Country Called Nigeria*.

Chief Abiola's senior wife and her driver were assassinated while on their way to discuss her husband's situation with the Canadian High Commission in June 1996. Many Nigerians, especially the Yoruba ethnic group felt that the military head of state, General Abacha, was responsible for her death, but fearing they might meet the same fate, they decided to suffer in silence.

Fela Ransome Kuti, a popular Nigerian musician known for his social activism and his marriage to twenty-seven women at the same time, died of AIDS in 1997. Fela's death brought Nigeria's attention to the deadly AIDS virus, which was moving across the continent as though it had a license to kill. Unfortunately, the fight against AIDS would not become a national priority in Nigeria until President Obasanjo addressed the problem in 1999.

In August 1996, Senator Moseley-Braun made a personal visit to Nigeria, and with the exception of associating with General Abacha's regime, there was not much to say about her visit.

In Nigeria's attempts to please the different ethnic groups who felt marginalized from the nation-building process, governments have tried to provide more states and local governments. This ongoing appeasing policy has now reached thirty-seven states, including the federal capital, without any success. Unfortunately, adding new states, local governments, and even relocating the federal capital from Lagos to Abuja was not going to help solve Nigeria's problems. When I made my first trip to Nigeria in 1978, there were only twelve states, and prior to that, the country had only four regions (east, midwest, north, and west). The different ethnic groups feel the best period of their fragile union was when the country had four regions prior to the civil war (1960-1967). The major reason for this was that the four regions had more control of their respective regions, which included 50 percent control of their natural resources and revenues.

Abacha continued his roundup of those he perceived as a threat to his dictatorial rule, and his latest victim was his second in command, General Diya, and five other high-ranking officers were accused of plotting a coup in December 1997. Like other Nigerian military tribunals, the military officers were tried, convicted, and condemned to death. However, through international pressure, their sentences were later overturned to twenty-five years. In the same month, General Yar'Adua (northerner), who was also perceived as a threat to Abacha, died while serving a life sentence in a federal prison.

Abacha paused from his wholesale looting of the country's treasury and promised a handover to an elected democratic civilian government in October of 1998. It was obvious that Abacha was preparing to hand over power to himself because the five government-sponsored political parties all had him as their presidential candidate. However, before this political scheme could take place, Abacha's death was announced in June 1998. There was some suspicion as to how Abacha met his death, but the military attributed his demise to a heart attack. Nigerians celebrated his death and once again took to the streets to express their momentary joy.

The new military leader, General Abubakar, who was also a northerner, showed signs of goodwill by immediately dismissing all charges against political prisoners detained by the Abacha regime, including Generals Obasanjo and Diya. He also released the constitution that Abacha had put on hold and allowed the formation of political parties and elections. He encouraged the release of Chief Abiola, but unfortunately Chief Abiola died in July 1998 of a heart attack while discussing the terms of his release with the military regime and the U.S. undersecretary of state Thomas Pinkering. Unfortunately, Chief Abiola tried to get his presidential mandate from a dictator who was determined to keep him in detention.

Since the military was running the country the majority of the time, it was not surprising that three former military heads of states were contesting to be Nigeria's next civilian president. The three generals were Buhari (north), Obasanjo (west), and Ojukwu (east), the former leader of Biafra. Out of the three generals, Ojukwu caught my attention because he fought against the other two generals during the Nigerian Civil War. Unfortunately, Ojukwu's misfortunes from the tragic civil war continued to follow him as he tried unsuccessfully to become the country's president. He blamed his latest misfortunes on some retired generals, who were still upset over his pardon by the Shagari government.

In March 1999, Obasanjo was able to withstand accusations of voting irregularities and deadly political violence to win the presidential elections over Buhari. Although Obasanjo was a Christian from the west, the Muslim north felt comfortable with him because he fought on the side of the federal government to keep the east from seceding from Nigeria during the civil war. He also handed over power in 1979 to the northern-led political party in the controversial presidential elections. The situation was not the same in his own western region, where his Yoruba kinsmen had not forgiven him for handing power over to a northerner the first time.

In August 2000, President Clinton made a two-day visit to Nigeria, becoming the second American president to visit the country since its independence in 1960. It was because of Abacha's dictatorial regime and human rights abuses that Nigeria was not included in Clinton's twelve-day visit to seven African nations in 1998. He was now visiting the country in an effort to show U.S. support by offering ten million dollars for the fight against HIV/AIDS. Although the amount the Clinton administration offered was not enough to arrest the spread of AIDS, it did awaken the American people and the rest of the world to the deadly epidemic in Africa. During their discussions, Clinton urged President Obasanjo to take tougher steps in combating drug trafficking while Obasanjo urged Clinton to use his influence to cancel or at least reduce the country's twenty-eight-billion-dollar foreign debt to the industrialized countries.

As I continued to observe the events in Nigeria, the country's festering religious problems reached another boiling point, and before things could cool down, more than two thousand Nigerians lost their lives to the violence. Religious intolerance between the mainly Christian south and the Muslim north has long been one of Nigeria's major problems, and the last thing the country needed was another reason to increase tensions between the two religious groups. The religious violence in 2000 erupted from the introduction of Islamic criminal civil law under Muslim Sharia, which has been in northern Nigeria since the twelfth century, but since Nigeria's independence in 1960, it was primarily used for marriages, inheritance, and other noncriminal issues.

The latest religious violence occurred during the 2002 Miss World competition held in Nigeria's national capital in Abuja. What attracted the world's attention was the threat of some beauty contestants to pull out of the competition when a pregnant woman convicted of adultery was sentenced to death. This "divorced" thirty-year-old woman was convicted under the Sharia criminal law of becoming pregnant outside of marriage. The punishment for this crime fell under the same Sharia law for adultery, which was death by stoning. Other punishments under the Sharia law included the amputation of limbs for theft and flogging for drinking alcohol, fornication, prostitution, gambling, and other nonviolent crimes. With the fear of being tried and convicted under the Sharia criminal laws, Christians and other non-Muslims found themselves once again trying to flee from the north. Like past religious disturbances in the north, there was always a retaliatory response from Christians in the south, which resulted in more death and destruction.

The threat of executing the woman by stoning, combined with the lost of lives and destruction of property, forced the organizers of the Miss World contest to relocate to London. Fortunately for the convicted woman, human rights groups and the international community convinced the Sharia court to delay the stoning execution until the accused woman gave birth. After the birth, the Islamic criminal court displayed further compassion by reversing the death sentence and eventually setting the woman free.

In February 2002, the British prime minister, Tony Blair, made a low-key visit to West Africa to help address significant problems like failed governments, poverty, AIDS, and other diseases ravaging the continent. Nigeria was first on Blair's four-nation itinerary, which included Ghana, Sierra Leone, and Senegal. Unlike Blair's ancestors, who showed no concern in bringing Nigeria's different ethnic groups together in 1914, Blair displayed a sense of general concern by suggesting that he and other Western leaders pay more attention to the problems of Africa or risk renewed terrorism in their own countries. It is important to note that Blair's concerns for the African continent did not become known until after the United States suffered a terrorist attack on September 11, 2001, and his support for the U.S. invasion of Iraq.

On the political scene, Obasanjo was reelected for a second four-year term in 2003, but not without some controversy. Like the 1999 elections, the 2003 elections were complicated by a multitude of election irregularities that ranged from massive rigging to the stealing of ballot boxes. There was also the problem of the government abusing human rights by allowing political, ethnic, and religious violence that killed more than eight thousand Nigerians. However, Obasanjo was able to weather another deadly political storm and began his second term under the dark cloud of impending violence.

There was not much improvement in the economic sector; unemployment was still high, and none of the four oil refineries was operating well enough to keep up with local demands for gasoline and kerosene. In fact, the fuel situation was so bad that Nigeria was once again importing processed petroleum products.

In July 2003, while Nigeria was trying to survive its present crisis, President Bush began his five-day tour of Africa. Unfortunately, he came to Africa with some credibility problems, which began during his campaign for the U.S. presidency in 1999 when he stated that Africa would not be a priority in his administration. Adding to Bush's lack of credibility was his unnecessary invasion of Iraq, the U.S. withdrawal from a number of international treaties, which included Kyoto Protocol, International Court, and last but not least, the discredited allegation that Iraq was trying to obtain uranium from Niger.

The documents used to support the Niger allegations had glaring mistakes, including the wrong letterhead and the signature of the country's foreign minister. The forgery discrepancies were brought to the attention of the Bush administration by CIA envoy ambassador Joseph Wilson and the Niger government in February of 2002. But in September 2002, Tony Blair's British government reinforced these allegations by stating that Iraq was an immediate threat and that they were still trying to purchase uranium from an African country. The Bush administration repeated this recycled allegation to the American people and the rest of the world. Unfortunately, in the Bush administration's desperate attempt to find another reason to invade Iraq, they overlooked the Niger discrepancies, and it was not surprising that the African leaders welcomed him with even more caution.

Accompanying President Bush on his stopover tour were Secretary of State Colin Powell and National Security Advisor Condoleezza Rice, along with some government officials and corporate executives ready to cash in on Nigeria's oil and liquefied gas. In regards to Powell and Rice, their presence should have been enough to impress the African leaders, but like Bush, these two prominent African Americans also had credibility problems because of their misleading statements leading up to the war with Iraq.

President Bush's agenda included pledges for financial assistance for AIDS, fighting terrorism, conflicts in Sudan, Rwanda, and for Charles Taylor to step down as president of war-torn Liberia. Africa was suffering from several deadly diseases, but it was AIDS in particular that was depleting the population and orphaning a generation of children. Unlike the other treatable diseases in Africa, the deadly AIDS virus had suspicious origins and no cure. Out of the estimated forty million people who are infected with the AIDS virus worldwide, thirty million of them are in Africa.

In Bush's effort to show compassion and help fight the global war against AIDS, and other serious diseases like tuberculosis and malaria, he pledged to give fifteen billion dollars over the next five years. It was going to take more than a morality clause to stop a disease that was taking more than six thousand lives daily. In the meantime, the deadly disease continued to move through Africa, with the help of ignorance and a stigma that only encouraged a deadly silence.

To aid the African economies, Bush introduced his new financial assistance program called the Millennium Challenge Account, whereby the recipient nation had to display good governance and accountability before the United States would release the funds. I welcomed this financial program if for no other reason than accountability, but it was wrong and insincere for the Bush administration to insist on accountability when they were withdrawing from international organizations that could hold them accountable.

Regarding terrorism, Kenya and Tanzania had already suffered terrorist attacks from Al-Qaeda through U.S. Embassy bombings that killed over 250 people and injured thousands more between the two countries. The two African leaders were hoping Bush would pay them a condolence visit, but unfortunately, they were not included in the itinerary because of security reasons.

Armed conflicts continued to impede any meaningful progress on the African continent; and Sudan, Rwanda, and Liberia were examples of this. It was the war-torn country of Liberia and its president Charles Taylor that drew the attention of the Bush Administration. Taylor had not only fought a civil war in his country, but he was also indicted for war crimes by a United Nations tribunal for purportedly aiding Sierra Leonean rebels, who were fighting against the government of Sierra Leone. With pressure from the United States and other African leaders, Taylor was persuaded to step down after being provided with asylum in Nigeria. He would eventually try to escape from Nigeria, but he was captured trying to cross the border with Chad in 2006. He was escorted to Liberia and subsequently to Sierra Leon to face trial for war crimes.

In an effort to make Africa more self-sufficient in the agriculture sector, Bush introduced a controversial Generic Modified seed (GM). African farmers were reluctant to use the GM seeds for several reasons. Their first objection was the higher cost for the U.S. patented seed over the traditional seeds. Their second objection was that the GM seeds could only be used once. Finally, the African farmers were unwilling to get involved with the GM seeds in fear of losing their small share of the European markets. The Europeans were not confident that the chemically treated seeds were safe for consumption. Therefore, instead of encouraging African countries to become more self-sufficient in food production, Bush was encouraging the African continent to become more dependent.

Based on President Bush's attitude toward Africa, I was reluctant to comment on his stopover tour, but there were some events worthy of comment. Bush began his African tour in Senegal, and unlike President Clinton, Bush was greeted with subdued receptions and protests. While he was in the country, he visited the infamous Goree Island, one of the major locations where thousands of Africans were held in captivity before being shipped off in shackles to America. After Bush's tour of Goree Island, he gave a speech describing his displeasure of the slave trade and the associated problems surrounding it, but he fell short of apologizing for U.S. participation in the highest crime against humanity. Toward the end of Bush's visit to Africa, the secretary of state, Colin Powell, responded to a question in an interview on CNN's *Larry King Live* when he was asked if President Bush should have apologized for slavery. Powell stated in part:

> No, I don't think there was a necessity for America to apologize. The United States, when we came into being as a nation, slavery was there. It took us awhile to recognize that we could not live our Constitution truly, unless we eliminated slavery; and hundreds of thousand of young men fought a civil war to end slavery, and then it took us a long time to get rid of the vestiges of slavery, and we are still working on it to this very day. And so, the very fact that we have come this far and we're working so hard, that shows what we think about slavery. But I don't know that it was necessary for the president of the United States to come here and apologize for the sins of those who were responsible for slavery so many hundreds of years ago.

I wondered if this was another misquote, a misleading statement, or an excuse for U.S. presidents not to apologize for the evil deeds of their ancestors. It is important to note that African Americans are forgiving to a fault, and the majority of us are still willing to leave this social birthmark of American history behind us if we knew white mainstream America, and some disillusioned African Americans were willing to do the same. But when U.S. leaders find it difficult to apologize publicly for something that they knew was wrong, it leaves little hope in trying to heal the wounds of slavery, racism, and all the other problems associated with it.

In South Africa, President Bush met another lukewarm reception and protesters who opposed the invasion of Iraq to his disregard for international law. Three years prior to Bush's visit to Africa, President Mbeki stated that the mysterious AIDS disease was part of a Western conspiracy to depopulate Africa and that HIV did not cause AIDS. Fortunately, Mbeki has since changed his mind and is now supporting all efforts to combat the deadly disease. Timing was another problem of the Bush administration, and they displayed this by cutting off military aid to South Africa a week before Bush visited the country. The reason behind this decision was that South Africa refused to grant Americans immunity from prosecution by the International Criminal Court. It is important to note that Nelson Mandela was noticeably absent during Bush's visit to South Africa. This diplomatic snub came as no surprise after Mandela voiced strong opposition to Bush's invasion of Iraq.

After a few hours in South Africa, Bush and his entourage headed for the neighboring country of Botswana. President Bush reechoed his pledges in his short visits to Botswana and subsequently Uganda before heading for Nigeria.

Nigeria had just ended a general strike three days prior to Bush's visit. The government had been trying to remove a subsidy from the fuel pump price of gasoline. Nigerians have jealously defended this fuel subsidy since the Gowon government in 1973 introduced it. Nigerians felt this was the only benefit they could see coming from the government and the oil companies. Another reason Nigerians objected to the removal was because the majority of them viewed the subsidy removal as an open invitation for their corrupt leaders to misuse the funds. Unfortunately, the national subsidy also provided an opportunity for illegal dealers to smuggle this natural resource into neighboring countries for increased profits. Compounding the subsidy problem was the government's inability to keep the four refineries operational, which was due to constant breakdowns, corruption, lack of accountability, and poor management. The refinery problem was so acute that the Nigerian government had to import fuel for its domestic use. These preventable failures had forced the Nigerian government to offer joint ventures to foreign companies for the operation and maintenance of their four oil refineries.

President Obasanjo had the unique opportunity of hosting three U.S. presidents. He was the military head of state when President Carter visited the country in 1978. He was also the civilian president when President Clinton visited in 2000, and now he was ready to receive President Bush. Bush landed on a Friday night in Nigeria's capital city of Abuja under extremely tight security, and once again, he met subdued protest. After a brief welcoming ceremony by President Obasanjo, his entourage was taken to the country's premier Nicon Hilton Hotel. The next morning Bush and his wife visited the national hospital for HIV/AIDS patients where Bush made his final pledge to help fight HIV/AIDS in Nigeria.

While Bush was in Nigeria, he addressed the sixth Leon Sullivan Summit, which was formerly known as the African-American Summit. The Sullivan Summit was established to help provide assistance to African countries regarding education, business development, investments and technical support. Mr. Leon Sullivan died in 2001; but his wife, Mrs. Grace Sullivan, was on hand along with other African dignitaries, including President Obasanjo, former United Nations Ambassador Andrew Young, congressional representative William Jefferson and other U.S. government dignitaries. Also in attendance were oil executives from Chevron-Texaco, Exxon-Mobil, and Royal Dutch Shell. Nigeria is Africa's largest supplier of oil and a member of OPEC (Organization of Petroleum Exporting Countries). OPEC was established in 1960 by oil-producing Middle Eastern countries to protect their interests against the major oil companies. Nigeria joined OPEC in 1971, and there were rumors that they were planning to leave OPEC, but the rotating chairman of the organization, who also happened to be a Nigerian, said they would remain an active member of the oil cartel. After spending less than twenty-four hours in Nigeria, Bush returned to the United States, and with the exception of pledging fifteen billion dollars for the global war against AIDS, he did very little to improve his credibility and his image toward Africa.

Oil continues to be a curse rather than a blessing to the people of Nigeria, particularly in the oil-producing areas. Over 90 percent of Nigeria's national revenues are still coming from the oil-producing areas in the midwest and east, yet they are among the most neglected communities in the country. These revenue-generating communities continue to suffer not only from the lack of basic services but also environmental hazards such as oil spills, soil, and river degradation, and over forty years of environmental gas flaring.

Unlike the Ogoni crisis where the weapons of choice were protests and boycotts, the crisis in 2004 involved an armed militia group called the Nigeria Delta Peoples Volunteer Force (NDPVF), which was based in the oil rich Niger Delta (midwest) and used violent tactics. Their methods included sabotage, hostage taking, the illegal tapping of pipelines, and other actions designed to get the attention of the Nigerian government and force it to address the deplorable conditions in the oil-producing areas. Asari, the leader of the NDPVF and a member of the Ijaw community, the largest ethnic group in the Niger Delta area, stated that all oil companies including Shell and Chevron should stop operation and leave the country until the NDPVF's demands were met. In addition to these demands, Asari called for a sovereign national conference.

Nigeria has been having national conferences since 1957, and they all have failed. The major reason for this is because the federal government has never allowed the delegates to discuss anything regarding the unity of the country. The government's failure to address this problem has led to civil war and misunderstanding among the ethnic major groups, especially between the Hausas in the north and the Ibos in the east. It was unfortunate how Nigerian governments and oil companies were taking the natural resources from the oil-producing areas and leaving them devastated and poor in the process.

Like past disruptions of Nigeria's crude oil production, Asari's protests managed to get the attention of the present government. Obasanjo invited the militia leader to the federal capital to have talks about the current crisis that was threatening Nigeria's economic lifeline. Although their meeting failed to produce the desired results that Asari and the people of the oil-producing areas had hoped for, it did produce an uneasy calm. But the fragile peace did not last long, Asari was arrested and put on trial for treason in September 2005.

If the Nigerian government thought by hanging the Ogoni leaders in 1995, and arresting Asari in 2005 that it was going to put an end to the demands from the oil-producing communities, they were mistaken. In February 2007, CNN's African correspondent Jeff Koinange did a special assignment on the militants in the oil-rich Niger Delta. The militant group identified themselves as the Movement for the Emancipation of the Niger Delta (MEND), and it once again brought world's attention to the plight of the oil-producing communities. Like Asari's Niger Peoples Volunteer Force, MEND was using all means available, which included foreign hostage taking, taking on the Nigerian armed forces, and helping to drive up the price of oil. Unfortunately, this was another example of oil being more of curse than a blessing to the people of Nigeria. Compounding the oil problems and the violence were the fuel pipeline explosions, which were a result of illegal tapping of fuel pipelines. Thousands of Nigerians lost their lives from these accidental explosions, as they were trying to take a share of this illegal bonanza.

When the leadership of a country is void of any accountability, it allows for other nonaccountable influences to enter at will. This was the case with Halliburton and Nigeria. Halliburton was already under investigation for contract violations in Iraq. And now they were under investigation for reportedly bribing Nigerian officials with over 180 million dollars to get an eight-billion-dollar government contract. Nigeria had been flaring gas since they discovered oil in 1957, but the bribe scandal cast doubt on the government's ability harness this natural resource and on their efforts to control the environmental impact on the oil-producing communities. After the alleged bribe was exposed in 2002, which began during the Abacha regime, the Obasanjo government suspended all activities with the company.

In June 2005, the world's richest industrialized countries, better known as the G8 (Britain, Canada, France, Germany, Italy, Japan, Russia, United States), and other lending institutions canceled the debts of eighteen of the world's poorest countries. Unsurprisingly, fourteen of these indebted countries were in sub-Saharan Africa, and it was easy to see why Nigeria, in spite of its natural resources, made the list of the poorest countries. Prior to the debt relief, countries were paying from 30 to 50 percent of their national revenues toward their never-ending debts. President Obasanjo and other African leaders brought it to the world's attention that the African countries could no longer afford to pay these amounts and survive. Prime Minister Blair successfully led and supported the debt issue with the other G8 members.

While African nations were enjoying their relief from debt that was incurred by some of the past and present leaders in 2006, Nigeria once again made the news in a negative way. This news in 2007 involved U.S. congressman William Jefferson, who was under an FBI investigation for alleged public corruption and bribing a high-ranking foreign official. According to the FBI reports that foreign official was Nigeria's vice president, Atiku Abubakar. Jefferson, who represents the majority of New Orleans and the unfortunate victims of Hurricane Katrina, denied the FBI allegations. Nigeria's vice president denied any wrongdoing with the embattled congressman. In 2007, Jefferson was indicted on sixteen counts, which included racketeering, wire fraud, money laundering, obstruction of justice, and eleven other counts. Regardless of the outcome of Jefferson's trial, his credibility had been challenged.

In April of 2007, Nigeria held its presidential election, and it was considered by national and international monitors as the country's worst. But the Obasanjo government overlooked these glaring irregularities as Nigeria had reached another crisis in their stormy attempts to govern to what many Nigerians consider to be an ungovernable country. I found it interesting that General Obasanjo handed over power to a northern president in the controversial elections of 1979, and now he was handing over to a northern president in another controversial presidential election in 2007.

The time has come to end these after notes, and it is my sincere hope that the people of Nigeria will come to some type of agreement that will allow them to coexist with each other. Their multiple marriage of inconvenience has led to nothing but unnecessary suffering and a tragic loss of lives. The people who make up Nigeria can no longer suffer in silence, and one of the ways of expressing their concerns is through a national conference. It is also important that the national conference take into consideration the social and cultural concerns of the different ethnic groups, instead of how they were brought together by the British in 1914.

Index

W

Y

References for the manuscript

Books

1. *Peoples and Empires of West Africa* (1971)
   Authors: G.T. Stride and C. Ifeka
   Publishers: Thomas Nelson and Sons Ltd. Mayfield Road, Walton
   London, England
2. *The Rise of the Nation States* (1965)
   Author: F. Abgodeka
   Publisher: Africana Educational Publishers (Nig) Ltd. London, England
3. *Nigeria*: Yesteday, Today, And . . . ?
   Author James O. Ojiako
   Publisher: Africana Educational Publishers (Nig) Ltd 79 Awka Road,
   P.M.B. 1639, Onitsha, Nigeria
4. *The Military in Politics* (1993)
   Edited by Dickson Agedah
   Publisher: Percetion Communications Limited, Plot 22, Jalupon Close
   Surulere, Lagos, Nigeria

Magazines

1. *Newswatch*
   Newswatch Communications Limited, No. 3 Billings Way, Oregun Industrial
   Estate, Oregun, P.M.B. 21499 Lagos, Nigeria
2. *Tell*
   Tell Communications Ltd, Textile Labour House, 10 Acme Road, P.M.B.
   21749. Ikeja, Nigeria
3. *New Yorker* (U.S.)